U.S. Fish & Wildlife Service

Crescent Lake
National Wildlife Refuge

*Comprehensive
Conservation Plan*

CCPs provide long-term guidance for management decisions and set forth goals, objectives, and strategies needed to accomplish refuge purposes and identify the Service's best estimate of future needs. These plans detail program planning levels that are sometimes substantially above current budget allocations and, as such, are primarily for Service strategic planning and program prioritization purposes. The plans do not constitute a commitment for staffing increases, operational and maintenance increases, or funding for future land acquisition.

Crescent Lake
National Wildlife Refuge

Comprehensive Conservation Plan

September 2002

Prepared by
U.S. Fish and Wildlife Service
Crescent Lake/North Platte National Wildlife Refuge Complex
115 Railway Street, Suite C109
Scottsbluff, NE 69361-3190

and

Crescent Lake National Wildlife Refuge
10630 Road 181
Ellsworth, NE 69340-6801

Approved: _Ralph O. Morgenweck_   _8/19/02_
Regional Director, Region 6, Denver, Colorado   Date

Crescent Lake National Wildlife Refuge
Comprehensive Conservation Plan Approval
U.S. Fish and Wildlife Service, Region 6

Submitted By:

Steven A. Knode
Project Leader
Crescent Lake National Wildlife Refuge Complex

August 12, 2002

Date

Concur:

Ron Cole
Refuge Program Supervisor

8-15-02

Date

Richard A. Coleman, Ph.D.
Regional Chief
National Wildlife Refuge System

8/15/02

Date

Summary

Crescent Lake National Wildlife Refuge is located in Garden County on the eastern edge of the Nebraska Panhandle. It lies on the southwestern edge of the 19,300 square mile Nebraska Sandhills, the largest sand dune area in the Western Hemisphere and one of the largest grass-stabilized regions in the world. The Sandhills are characterized by rolling, vegetated hills and inter-dunal valleys which are oriented in a northwest to southeast direction. Many shallow lakes and marshes are interspersed in the lower valleys. Native grasses predominate. Wildlife diversity, except large ungulates and their predators, is relatively unchanged since early settlement.

There are 21 wetland complexes on the Refuge totaling approximately 8,251 acres or about 18 percent of the total area. These wetlands are a mixture of shallow lakes, marshes, seasonal wetlands, wet meadows and a small stream resulting from Refuge management activities.

The Sandhills are within a wide transitional zone called the Mixed Grass Prairie which lies between Tallgrass Prairie to the east and Short Grass Prairie to the west. Although precipitation is typical of the semi-arid Mixed Grass Prairie, the Sandhills are characterized by post-climax, tallgrass species typical of a greater moisture regime (Oosting 1948; Keeler, et al 1980).

The Nebraska Sandhills are one of the few large native prairie areas in the United States that have not been substantially converted to farmland or otherwise modified. Thus, most of the plant and animal species present when settlement began are still present today.

This is a 15-year Plan, but only the goals will remain static. Objectives and strategies are based on present knowledge and reflect known needs. They may change, as may specific management actions, as knowledge and needs change. Public involvement will be sought for any significant amendments.

It is also important to understand that individual objectives cannot be taken out of context. It is the mixture of objectives that will produce the desired results. Generally speaking, on Crescent Lake Refuge, where the legal mandate is to serve as a "refuge and breeding ground for birds and other wild animals," habitat is managed to support or produce birds and other wildlife. However, because it is the habitat over which wildlife managers have most control, a clear understanding must also occur of the kinds and amounts of habitat needed to support that wildlife. Public use and environmental education are also important functions of the Refuge. Thus, it is important to know what kinds and how much public use can be allowed and remain compatible with the wildlife purposes and objectives.

The main goals of the CCP are:

Endangered, Threatened, and Candidate Species
- *Goal: Contribute to the preservation and restoration of endangered flora and fauna that are or were endemic to the Crescent Lake Refuge area.*

Upland Habitat
- *Goal: Preserve, restore, and enhance the ecological diversity of indigenous flora and fauna of the physiographic region described as the Sandhills Prairie.*

Wilderness
- *Goal: Preserve, restore, and enhance the ecological diversity of indigenous flora and fauna of the physiographic region described as the Sandhills Prairie, while maintaining and enhancing the wilderness quality.*

Wetland Habitat
- *Goal: Maintain natural and artificially managed permanent and semipermanent wetlands to provide habitat for migratory waterfowl, shorebirds, wading birds, and associated wetland-dependent species.*

Fish and Wildlife
- *Goal: Preserve, restore, and enhance the ecological diversity and abundance of migratory birds and other indigenous fish and wildlife with emphasis on grassland-dependent species.*

Interpretation and Recreation
- *Goal: Provide visitors an opportunity to enjoy, learn about and utilize fish and wildlife in a setting that emphasizes an undisturbed natural environment and minimum human interaction.*

Community Involvement / Support Systems
- *Goal: Interact with communities and organizations to create mutually beneficial partnerships.*

Meadowlark © Cindie Brunner

Table of Contents

IV. Refuge Goals, Objectives, and Strategies

V. Implementation and Monitoring

Environmental Action Statement

Finding of No Significant Impact (FONSI)

Appendices

Maps

Figures

Purpose and Vision

Legal Purpose

Crescent Lake National Wildlife Refuge was established on March 16, 1931, by Executive Order 5597 which defined the legal purpose as an area "... reserved and set apart ... as a refuge and breeding ground for birds and wild animals."

It is important to understand this legal purpose, particularly because it includes all wild animals, not just migratory birds. It is the hub around which planning, management actions, and compatibility determinations revolve.

Vision

> "I am the grass; I cover all ...
> "I am the grass
>   Let me work"
>   - Carl Sandberg (Grass)

A sea of grass in a sea of grass, Crescent Lake National Wildlife Refuge was established primarily for the concentration of native prairie and associated wetlands which, together, attract a wide variety of wildlife, particularly migratory birds. But, like all national wildlife refuges, Crescent Lake Refuge is not an island, independent of what goes on around it. It is part of larger and dynamic social, economic and biological communities, communities that also affect wildlife that use the Refuge. Unlike many Refuges, however, surrounding land use, principally cattle grazing, is relatively stable, public use is relatively low, and there are few threats from the outside.

Thus, we envision a Refuge about the same size it is now, the purpose of which is to maintain in perpetuity a representative sample of the native prairie and wildlife associated with this part of the Nebraska Sandhills. We see habitat in excellent condition, fewer exotic plants, and a healthy and growing population of blowout penstemon, an endangered plant. We see a visiting public which values the solitude and for which relatively few but high quality learning and recreational facilities are available. We see about half of the Refuge as a National wilderness area which supports bison, a species not present in the area in a wild state for over 100 years. We see the Refuge doing its part to support migratory birds enjoyed by people in States up and down the Central Flyway. We see active partnerships with surrounding landowners to help them maintain habitat on private lands while engaged in sustained, profitable agriculture. We see the Refuge as a contributing part of the Nebraska Sandhills.

I. Introduction / Background

Purpose of a Comprehensive Conservation Plan

The National Wildlife Refuge System Improvement Act of 1997 requires that Comprehensive Conservation Plans (CCP) be prepared for each unit of the National Wildlife Refuge System, and that the public be involved in preparing and revising these plans.

Comprehensive planning creates an opportunity to meet with neighbors, customers, and other agencies to identify and discuss natural resource issues and help ensure the plan meets the changing needs of wildlife and people. This Plan discusses history, goals and objectives, and the general direction refuge management will take over the next 15 years. For a complete discussion of the planning process, refer to the "Draft Planning Policy Pursuant to the National Wildlife Refuge System Improvement Act of 1997" (copies available at the Refuge Headquarters).

Refuge History - an Overview
Establishment and Administration

The 45,849-acre Crescent Lake National Wildlife Refuge (Refuge), established in 1931, is located 28 miles north of Oshkosh, Nebraska in Garden County at the southwestern end of the Nebraska Sandhills (Map 1). It is administered by the U.S. Fish & Wildlife Service (Service) as part of the Crescent Lake/North Platte National Wildlife Refuge Complex, and is within the Central Flyway. The Complex headquarters is 100 miles to the west in the City of Scottsbluff.

The initial Refuge was 36,920 acres, acquired primarily from one large ranch. Additional lands were acquired between 1932 and 1937. Most lands were acquired or exchanged under the authority of the Migratory Bird Conservation Act (45 Stat. 1222). About 2,566 acres were acquired under the Resettlement Administration (Executive Order 7027, April 30, 1935), a drought and depression relief program.

The Nebraska Sandhills were settled largely as a result of the Kincaid Act of 1904, a modification of the Homestead Act to allow settlers 640 acres in "less productive" areas. As a result, a homestead existed in almost every meadow. However, 640 acres was not a viable farm/ranch unit in the Sandhills, and land was soon consolidated into larger units. Today, the Sandhills are home to some of the largest ranches in the country. Because of the large acreage required to support economically viable units, Garden County is among the least densely populated areas in the continental United States. Most of the Refuge location names originated from the early homesteaders.

The earliest government actions on the Refuge were tree plantings and small construction projects by the Civilian Conservation Corps (CCC) and the Works Projects Administration (WPA). The CCC built several buildings still in use today at the Refuge headquarters. The WPA built roads, fences, and other facilities, such as the fire tower and buildings, at the headquarters site.

Initially, the staff at Crescent Lake Refuge was also responsible for the 2,909-acre North Platte Refuge, 100 miles to the west. The latter was not staffed until 1990 when the Crescent Lake/North Platte National Wildlife Refuge Complex was officially formed. The Complex headquarters was moved to Scottsbluff in 1993.

All lands around the Refuge are in private ownership except for a small ranch on the west boundary, purchased in 1984 by The Nature Conservancy for preservation of the blowout penstemon (an endangered plant). The only other public land in Garden County is Ash Hollow State Historical Park, 50 miles to the southeast. In March 2000, media entrepreneur Ted Turner purchased a large ranch adjacent to the east boundary of the Refuge; plans for this area are not yet known, although Mr. Turner has placed bison on holdings in Nebraska, Montana, and other states.

Because of its remote location, the Refuge must provide housing for employees. Currently, housing is available for five permanent and four temporary employees. Four service and equipment storage buildings, together with the residences, are clustered in a compact headquarters area (Map 2). Additional equipment storage and two buildings are located across the county road about one-half mile to the east.

Wildlife and Habitat Management

Special Places In 1972, a 24,502-acre area was proposed for inclusion in the National Wilderness Preservation System (Map 2). Although Congress has not acted on the proposal, no development has occurred in the area since 1972.

Two Research Natural Areas were established in 1955 by a Director's Order and included on the National List of Research Areas (Map 2). The Goose Lake RNA (940 acres) has not been grazed, hayed, or intentionally burned since 1948. The Hackberry Lake RNA (172 acres) has not been disturbed since 1951, except for a 60-acre spring burn in 1983 and a short duration spring graze in 1988.

Populations Management Direct populations management consisted primarily of providing sanctuary and controlling predators. Predator control was a significant management activity until 1994, when is was suspended due to staffing limitations and modest results. Public trapping has occurred sporadically. It ended in 1954 when it became economically unfeasible, was revived in the 1980s, but again faded out with low fur prices.

Wetland Management The Refuge has about 8,250 acres of wetlands; there are no permanent natural streams. Manipulation of water levels is possible only on nine lakes and has been used to control shoreline vegetation and create open shoreline for migratory birds. Pothole blasting occurred in the late 1960s to create additional waterfowl breeding habitat; results were limited and the effort was discontinued after a few years. Natural filling of wetlands and invasion of phragmites, an exotic plant, are emerging problems.

Upland Management The agreement for purchase of the original 36,920 acres allowed previous owners to continue to graze at no cost for 10 years. The only restriction was that no more than 4,000 cattle could be on the Refuge at any one time. By the end of the 10 years, most of the Refuge was seriously overgrazed. During World War II, the Refuge was leased to surrounding ranches for cattle grazing to help meet wartime needs. Although the stocking rate then was half that on surrounding commercial lands, Refuge grasslands made little recovery. After the War, grazing gradually declined.

Although the Refuge has largely recovered from overgrazing in the past, grazing remains an important tool. Today, native prairie management consists of a combination of rest, grazing, and prescribed burning. Prescribed burning was first used as a management tool in 1984 and has obvious limitations in this sea of grass; about 500 acres are planned for burning annually.

Noxious weeds are a ubiquitous problem, and the Refuge is no exception. Fortunately, surrounding private lands are well-managed and the problem is limited to Canada thistle. Leafy spurge was eradicated from the Refuge in 1994.

There are about 80 acres of trees on the Refuge, most of which were planted by the CCC in the 1930s. Trees add diversity; however, with the exception of cottonwoods and willows, they are not a normal part of the Sandhills Prairie. There is no active management and the acreage is steadily declining through natural mortality.

Cultural Resources

Historic, archaeological, and paleontological resources are protected by
Federal laws. No formal, systematic cultural resource surveys have been
onducted on the Refuge. The buildings constructed by the CCC or WPA are
more than 50 years old and qualify for preservation.

Public Use

Recreation and Education Portions of the Refuge have always been open for
hunting, fishing, wildlife observation, and general nature-oriented activities.
A Special Use Permits can be used to allow the public to trap. The Refuge is
isolated (Oshkosh, population 1,100, is the nearest town and 28 miles away)
and accessible by few and relatively rough roads. This isolation limits the
number of visitors but is an important and desirable quality for most who do
come. Public use averages about 8,000 visitors per year.

Facilities were always minimal and, even today, are limited to one auto tour
route, two graveled boat ramps, two fishing piers, a public rest room,
modest interpretive displays at the headquarters, and kiosks at the
entrances.

Originally, Refuge lakes did not contain sport fish. Today, three lakes
support sport fisheries which are used by over 5,000 anglers annually. The
Nebraska Game and Parks Commission (NGPC) manages sport fisheries
with concurrence of the refuge manager.

Hunting has always occurred on the Refuge and has grown to about 600
visits per year.

Economic Use As mentioned above, the Refuge was heavily grazed until the
mid-1940s. Since about 1970, grazing has been considered a tool for wildlife
management and the amount of grazing declined as grassland improved and
native prairie conditions were restored. The current practice of grazing the
meadows 1 year out of 6 and the uplands 1 year out of 20 was initiated in
1993. In the past, as many as 20 permittees grazed cattle on the Refuge
annually and the amount of grazing exceeded 24,000 animal unit months
(AUMs). Today, only 3 to 5 permittees use the Refuge in any given year and
grazing is limited to about 2,500 AUMs. Grazing fees are established
through competitive bidding and are lower than those in much of the
Sandhills because Refuge grazing areas are difficult to access.

The National Wildlife Refuge System
Mission and Goals and Guiding Principles

The National Wildlife Refuge System (Refuge System) is the world's largest collection of lands set aside specifically for wildlife. The first unit of the System, a 3-acre pelican and heron rookery in Florida, was created in 1903 by President Theodore Roosevelt. Today, the System includes nearly 540 national wildlife refuges, thousands of small wetlands and other special management areas encompassing more than 95 million acres and located in all 50 States and a number of U.S. Territories.

The Refuge System provides habitat for endangered species, migratory birds, species of management concern (see Glossary and Appendix H) and other "trust resources" for which the Federal government is ultimately responsible. It also provides habitat for resident wildlife and offers wildlife-dependent recreation for over 34 million visitors annually.

Fish and Wildlife Service Mission

"To work with others to conserve, protect, and enhance fish and wildlife and plants and their habitats for the continuing benefit of the American people."

To fulfill this mission, Congress has charged the Service with conserving and managing migratory birds, endangered species, anadromous and interjurisdictional fish, and certain marine mammals. The Service carries out these responsibilities through several functional entities, one of which is the National Wildlife Refuge System.

National Wildlife Refuge System Mission

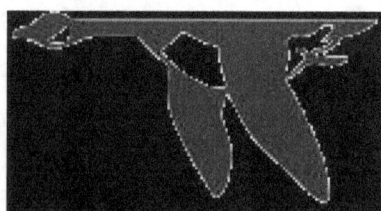

This goose, designed by J.N. "Ding" Darling, has become the symbol of the National Wildlife Refuge System.

"To administer a national network of lands and waters for the conservation, management, and where appropriate, restoration of the fish, wildlife, and plant resources and their habitats within the United States for the benefit of present and future generations of Americans" (National Wildlife Refuge System Improvement Act of 1997, Public Law 105-57).

National Wildlife Refuge System Goals

1. *To fulfill our statutory duty to achieve refuge purpose(s) and further the System mission.*
2. *Conserve, restore where appropriate, and enhance all species of fish, wildlife, and plants that are endangered or threatened with becoming endangered.*
3. *Perpetuate migratory bird, interjurisdictional fish, and marine mammal populations.*
4. *Conserve a diversity of fish, wildlife, and plants.*
5. *Conserve and restore, where appropriate, representative ecosystems of the United States, including the ecological processes characteristic of those ecosystems.*
6. *To foster understanding and instill appreciation of fish, wildlife, and plants, and their conservation, by providing the public with safe, high-quality, and compatible wildlife-dependent public use. Such use includes hunting, fishing, wildlife observation and photography, and environmental education and interpretation.*

While individual refuges are important in and of themselves, they are even more important for their collective benefits as a network. Together, national wildlife refuges form a network of lands spanning the entire continent - supporting birds migrating from Alaska and Canada to the southern States and points south, preserving trust resources, and providing enjoyment for people throughout the United States and neighboring countries. Together, they help prevent species from becoming threatened or endangered by securing habitat in all or portions of a species range. Thus, the network is critical - a deficiency in one location may affect wildlife in other locations.

Legal and Policy Guidance

National wildlife refuges are guided by: The mission and goals of the National Wildlife Refuge System; the legal purpose of the specific refuge unit as described in the establishing legislation or executive orders; International Treaties; Federal laws and regulations; and Service policies. Key concepts and guidance for the System are included in the National Wildlife Refuge System Administration Act of 1966, The Refuge Recreation Act of 1962, Title 50 of the Code of Federal Regulations, the Fish and Wildlife Service Manual, Executive Order 12996 (March 23, 1996) and, most recently, the National Wildlife Refuge System Improvement Act of 1997. Appendix C contains a partial list of Federal laws governing administration of the System.

Crescent Lake Refuge is also guided by a number of agreements with other agencies and by the conditions presented in the Environmental Assessment (published with the Draft CCP) and Compatibility Determinations (Appendix E).

Important Concepts for Management of National Wildlife Refuges

Compatibility. "Compatibility" is an important legal concept. The National Wildlife Refuge System Administration Act of 1966 allowed public use of any area within the System, provided that such use was "compatible" with the major purposes for which such areas were established. The concept was further defined and strengthened by the National Wildlife Refuge System Act of 1997. Thus, by law, all uses of national wildlife refuges, including land management activities and wildlife-dependent recreation, must be formally determined to be "compatible." A compatible use is defined as one that, in the professional judgement of the refuge manager, will not materially interfere with or detract from the fulfillment of the mission of the System or the purposes of the refuge. Professional judgement is further defined as a determination that is consistent with sound fish and wildlife management and administration practices, available science, available resources (including funding, personnel, facilities, and other infrastructure), and adherence with applicable laws. See Appendix E for a synopsis of compatibility determinations for the major uses allowed on Crescent Lake Refuge.

Wildlife as Priority. The National Wildlife Refuge System Improvement Act of 1997 states that wildlife conservation is the priority of the System. It amends the Refuge System Administration Act by including a unifying mission for the System, a formal process for determining compatible uses, and a requirement that each refuge will be managed under a Comprehensive Conservation Plan. Further, the Act defines wildlife-dependent recreational uses as: hunting and fishing, wildlife observation and photography, environmental education and interpretation. (Specific details regarding these and other amendments are available through the Refuge or Regional Office.)

Partnerships and Public Involvement. Executive Order 12996 (March 23, 1996) also provides important guidance. Among other things it: stresses the importance of partnerships with Federal and State agencies, Tribes, organizations, industry, and the general public; and, mandates public involvement in decisions on acquisition and management of refuges.

Existing Partnerships

Partnerships with local, State and Federal Agencies, private conservation organizations, and landowners are important not only for achieving and sustaining Refuge objectives but to assure the Refuge is an active member of the community and contributes to the broader objectives of that community. Existing partnerships include:

- Nebraska Game and Parks Commission - Fisheries and wildlife management/Law enforcement
- University of Nebraska - Blowout penstemon recovery
- Earlham University - Reptile and amphibian research
- Central Panhandle Mutual Aid Association - Fire suppression and other emergencies
- The Nature Conservancy - Blowout penstemon recovery
- North Platte Valley Sportmans Association - National Fishing Day activities
- Natural Resource Conservation Service - Wetland Reserve Program
- National Weather Service - Weather station data
- Nebraska National Forest - Interagency Fire Agreement
- U.S. Geological Survey - Water resources management
- Local landowners - FWS Partners for Fish and Wildlife Program

II. Planning Process

Description

The project leader for the Crescent Lake/North Platte National Wildlife Refuge Complex and the manager of the Crescent Lake Refuge were assigned primary responsibility for planning in May 1998. An open house/ scoping session was held in Oshkosh on July 16, 1998, to inform the public of the planning process and to seek ideas on Refuge programs and issues. About 150 invitations were mailed to local and national stakeholders (educators, permittees, neighbors, other agencies and non-profit organizations). The general public was also invited through widely published/broadcast news releases. Information could also be obtained by contacting the Refuge Manager and comments could be submitted in writing.

Refuge staff also met personally with the Alliance Office of the Nebraska Game and Parks Commission (NGPC), Wildcat Audubon Society, the North Platte Valley Sportsmans Association, the Alliance Rotary Club and the Scottsbluff Lions Club to discuss the CCP process.

In November 1998, the Project Leader formed an interdisciplinary team to provide input and critical review (Appendix K).

The final CCP will guide management of the Crescent Lake Refuge for the next 15 years. It will be used to prepare and revise step-down management plans, performance plans, and budget requests. The Plan will be reviewed during routine Refuge inspections and programmatic evaluations. When changes are needed, the level of public involvement and associated NEPA documentation will be determined by the Project Leader. The entire plan will be formally reviewed and revised at least every 15 years.

Planning Assumptions / Limitations
Proposed Wilderness Area

The 24,502-acre proposed Wilderness Area, until accepted or rejected by Congress, must be managed as if it was wilderness; only "minimum tools" can be used (see Section IV and Appendix G).

Research Natural Areas

The two officially designated RNAs (1,076 acres) are to remain free of human disturbance, including habitat management and public use.

Planning Issues

The following issues were identified during the public scoping process and/or discussions with review team members. Some additional information is available in the Environmental Assessment (published with the Draft CCP).

Wilderness Proposal and Research Natural Areas

(see previous page)

Endangered Species

The Refuge is within the range of the blowout penstemon, a federally-listed endangered plant, and plays an important role in its survival.

Public Access

The Refuge is accessible only by relatively narrow, rough roads; most interior roads are passable only with four-wheel-drive vehicles.

Hunting and Fishing

The Refuge is open to deer and upland bird hunting but not waterfowl.

Invasive Species

Canada thistle exists in varying densities throughout the Refuge, including the Proposed Wilderness Area and Research Natural Areas. Phragmites is an aggressive wetland invader.

Bison Reintroduction

Bison were once part of the Sandhills Prairie ecosystem and should be considered for reintroduction into the Proposed Wilderness Area.

Lands of Interest

Several adjacent areas are potentially important for the endangered blowout penstemon, wetland values, and migratory birds and are candidates for additional protection.

Staffing and Funding

Several people expressed concern that funds would never be available to staff the Refuges and implement the Plan.

III. *Refuge and Resource Descriptions*

Socio-economic Environment

Crescent Lake Refuge is located in Garden County on the eastern edge of the Nebraska Panhandle, an 11-county, 14,000-square-mile region with a population of about 90,000 people. Basic economic activities in Garden County include irrigated and dryland farming, cattle feeding, and ranching.

According to the Nebraska Panhandle Economic Development Report (Panhandle Area Dev. Dist., undated ca. 1998), the population of Garden County decreased from 2,460 in 1990 to 2,224 in 1997, a decrease of about 10 percent. The population in the year 2010 is projected at 1,707, a decrease of more than 20 percent from 1997; similar trends are projected for much of the surrounding rural area. Only the major population centers, such as Scottsbluff/Gering (100 miles to the west), project growth of any significance.

Geographic / Ecosystem Setting

Crescent Lake Refuge lies on the southwestern edge of the 19,300 square mile Nebraska Sandhills, the largest sand dune area in the Western Hemisphere and one of the largest grass-stabilized regions in the world. The Sandhills are characterized by rolling, vegetated hills and inter-dunal valleys which are oriented in a northwest to southeast direction. Many shallow lakes and marshes are interspersed in the lower valleys. Native grasses predominate. Wildlife diversity, except large ungulates and their predators, is relatively unchanged since early settlement.

About 177,000 acres of open water lakes, shallow marshes and fens, and nearly 1,130,000 acres of wet meadows remain in the Sandhills. Most wetlands are freshwater; about 10 percent are alkaline. They range in size from 1 to 2,300 acres, but 80 percent are less than 10 acres (LaGrange 1997). Many wetlands have been drained in attempts to increase hay production. Estimates of the amount drained range from 15 percent (McMurtrey and Craig 1969) to 46 percent (USFWS 1986). Wetland drainage continues to this day (Bleed and Flowerday 1989).

The Fish and Wildlife Service operates under an "ecosystem approach to resource management" and, for organizational purposes, has identified watershed-based ecosystems. The Crescent Lake Refuge is within the Platte-Kansas Rivers Ecosystem (Map 3).

Climate

Climate of the Sandhills is characteristic of the central Great Plains - cold winters, hot summers, and frequent thunderstorms from spring to late summer. Annual precipitation ranges from 17 to 23 inches (Wilhite and Hubbard 1989), and is coupled with high evapo-transpiration rates. The Refuge has operated an official weather station since 1935. Precipitation on the Refuge averages 16.8 inches and temperatures have ranged from minus 46 to 109 degrees Fahrenheit. Since 1976, relatively high precipitation has resulted in positive net moisture balances (annual precipitation minus open pan evaporation) in most years.

Soils

Most soils are wind-laden sands that have not been held in place long by vegetation. They are light colored and have little organic matter. Soils in basins, valleys, and wet meadows have thicker and darker surface layers and more organic matter than soils found in the hills. The main soil types are dune sand, Valentine sands, Valentine-loamy sands, and Gannett loamy sands. Rainfall is quickly absorbed and causes little erosion; soil evaporation rates are low. Native grasses grow well under these conditions, but soil exposed by overgrazing or plowing is subject to wind erosion (Layton, et al 1956).

Geology

During the Cretaceous period of the Mesozoic era, a shallow sea covered the area of the Sandhills. When the sea receded, large valleys were formed which today are covered with sand. The geological processes are not well understood because of that sand cover. The exact time is debated, but somewhere between 4,000 and 8,000 years ago, water deposited sand which later began shifting as a result of climatic changes. This blowing sorted the alluvial deposits; fine material was carried out of the area and coarse material was left behind, resulting in the uniform particle size typical of wind deposited dunes (Bleed and Flowerday 1989).

Refuge Resources
Water and Wetlands

The Nebraska Sandhills overlay the High Plains Aquifer, commonly referred to as the Ogallala Aquifer. This groundwater is the source of wetlands in low areas and valleys and is the driving force supporting the ecological diversity and integrity of the Sandhills.

There are 21 wetland complexes on the Refuge totaling approximately 8,251 acres or about 18 percent of the total area (Map 4). These wetlands are a mixture of shallow lakes, marshes, seasonal wetlands, wet meadows and a small stream resulting from Refuge management activities. They were classified as follows by the Fish and Wildlife Service (USFWS, Sandhills Wetlands 1986):

Type II, Fresh Meadows	4,755 acres
Type III, Shallow Fresh Marshes	1,154 acres
Type IV, Fresh Marshes	309 acres
Type V, Open Fresh Water	2,033 acres

A few, small alkaline wetlands also exist. These were not specifically identified as such by the inventory and total about 413 acres. Submergent and emergent wetland vegetation ranges from sparse to dense depending on soils and alkalinity. Emergent vegetation includes cattail, bulrush, and phragmites. Vegetation bordering wetlands is primarily grasses and sedges. A few lakes have associated groves of cottonwood and willow trees, usually on the north shores.

Most Refuge wetlands rise and fall with precipitation and groundwater levels. Since 1981, precipitation has been above average resulting in record water levels. Control structures and elevation gauges have been installed on nine lakes, but water levels can be increased significantly on only five that are connected to a ditch which drains a private marsh north of the Refuge. Gauges on Island Lake record natural fluctuations. The U.S. Geological Survey has many groundwater survey wells on the Refuge which are used to study the complex groundwater hydrology of the area; the Refuge staff monitors about 25 of these.

Vegetation

The Sandhills are within a wide transitional zone called the Mixed Grass Prairie which lies between Tallgrass Prairie to the east and Short Grass Prairie to the west. Although precipitation is typical of the semi-arid Mixed Grass Prairie, the Sandhills are characterized by post-climax, tallgrass species typical of a greater moisture regime (Oosting 1948; Keeler, et al 1980). This is due primarily to the moisture penetration and holding capacities of the soil, root structures, and photosynthetic strategies of cool and warm season plants (Tolstead 1942; Barnes 1984).

The Refuge plant herbarium contains 223 species; however, the collection is incomplete (Appendix F).

Vegetative Types

Four basic vegetative types or range sites are on the Refuge (NRCS 1995). (see Map 4)

Wetland Range Sites. These low meadow sites make up only 1 percent of the Refuge and are dominated by species that thrive in a moisture-saturated soil profile, such as prairie cordgrass, blue-joint reed grass, sedge species, and non-grass species such as golden rod, dock, and willows.

Sub-irrigated Range Sites. These are meadows close to the groundwater level where soil moisture can support deep-rooted, warm season native grasses even during drought. They make up about 9 percent of the Refuge and are dominated by tallgrass species such as switchgrass and sand bluestem. They are also prone to invasion by exotic species, such as Kentucky bluegrass and smooth brome, and noxious weeds, such as Canada thistle.

Sand Range Sites. These include the dry meadows (the edge between wet meadows and the sandhills) and the gently undulating sandhills, They make up about 76 percent of the Refuge. Predominate grasses include both cool season species such as needle-and-thread and western wheatgrass, and warm season species such as prairie sandreed, sand bluestem, sand love grass, and sand dropseed. Common non-grass species include prairie sunflower, yucca, lead plant, and prairie rose. Exotic species, such as cheatgrass, will invade these sites.

Choppy Sand Range Sites. These are the characteristic dunes for which the Nebraska Sandhills are named and make up about 11 percent of the Refuge. They support a wide variety of vegetation but also contain many, relatively small, unvegetated areas, commonly called "blowouts," that are subject to wind erosion. The number of blowouts vary with terrain but, overall, these open sand areas make up about 3 percent of the choppy sand range sites. Blowout penstemon (*Penstemon haydenii*), a federally-listed endangered species, is endemic to the Sandhills and its characteristic habitat includes the blowouts and open sand areas. Predominate grasses include blue grama, sand bluestem, sand dropseed, blowout grass, sand love grass, little bluestem, and sandhills muhly. Non-grass species include yucca, sand cherry, prairie rose, and prairie sunflower.

Perennial and annual flowering forbs are an important component of true native prairie and are more abundant on the Refuge than on the surrounding private lands which are managed for livestock production. Although formal surveys are not conducted, refuge managers have observed an increase in non-grass species since grazing was reduced starting in 1993.

There are about 45 species of native and introduced trees and shrubs in the Sandhills, 30 of which occur on the Refuge. Some, such as sand sage, choke cherry, sandbar willow, and cottonwood, are characteristic of native prairie. Many are not. The Civilian Conservation Corps planted native and nonnative trees and shrubs during the 1930s, most of which have disappeared. Mature trees succumb to prairie fires and porcupines, and seedlings rarely survive deer and rodent browsing. The only tree species that has become successfully established without human assistance is the green ash which reproduces well but only in the shade canopy of mature willows or cottonwoods. There are about 80 acres of trees on the Refuge.

Endangered Plants

Hayden's, or blowout, penstemon is Nebraska's rarest plant (Farrar 1990) and the only endangered plant on the Refuge. It was placed on the Federal list of endangered species in 1987. This plant is somewhat unique in that it depends on non-vegetated sand surfaces, or blowouts, for its existence (Fritz, et al 1992). Good management of private grazing lands has reduced the amount of blowouts in the Sandhills; only in the drier western fringes are blowouts still common. In 1984, The Nature Conservancy purchased an 840-acre area adjacent to the Refuge specifically for perpetuation of blowout penstemon.

Blowout penstemon surveys began on the Refuge in 1987 when 2,058 plants were found. In 1998, only 415 remained (see Figure 1). Although shrinking habitat is part of the problem, plant populations are declining even in areas with what appears to be good habitat. So, other factors are at work. Perhaps genetic viability is failing as plants become increasingly isolated from each other. Since 1997, the University of Nebraska has supplied seedlings grown at a facility in Lincoln. About 9,500 plants have been planted on the Refuge through 2000; about 15 percent of the 1997 planting and 20 percent of the 1998 planting survived.

Figure 1. Penstemon Populations			
Year	Native	Surviving Transplants	Total
1987	2,058	--	2,058
1988	1,652	--	1,652
1989	1,264	--	1,264
1990	1,545	--	1,545
1991	765	--	765
1992	1,055	--	1,055
1993	985	--	985
1994	956	--	956
1995	624	--	624
1996	608	--	608
1997	533	332	865
1998	415	831*	1,246
1999	407	777**	1,184
2000	486	546***	1,032

* Includes 1998 transplants
** Does not include the 1999 transplants
*** Does not include the 2000 transplants

Plant Species of Management Concern

Plant Species of Management Concern listed by the U.S. Fish & Wildlife Service or the State of Nebraska are presented in Appendix H. In addition, there are several other plant species which will receive special management emphasis on Crescent Lake Refuge for the reasons listed below:

Canada thistle	Widespread noxious weed
Cheatgrass brome	Exotic, expanding range
Common reed	Exotic, expanding range
Eastern cottonwood	High wildlife values, native plant, decreasing range
Blowout penstemon	Federally-listed endangered species, decreasing range

Wildlife

The Nebraska Sandhills are one of the few large native prairie areas in the United States that have not been substantially converted to farmland or otherwise modified. Thus, most of the plant and animal species present when settlement began are still present today.

Surveys and census activities are limited by staffing and funding. Most are broad-scale sampling, which works well for large numbers of highly visible species but yields erratic and questionable results for species which are less visible or occur in smaller numbers. Some intensive, more sophisticated surveys have been discontinued because of insufficient staff and questionable data. As a result, high quality, refuge-specific information is not available for many species.

Endangered and Threatened Species

There are no federally-listed endangered wildlife which depend on the Refuge in any significant way. Prairie falcons, least terns, and piping plovers are occasionally seen during migrations but are considered casual visitors. The ferruginous hawk is considered a sensitive species but is an uncommon migrant. Black terns and loggerhead shrikes are also sensitive species which nest on the Refuge. Recent informal surveys revealed about 100 tern nests and 20 shrike nests.

The swift fox, an infrequent visitor, is a State-listed species for which little information is available. One sighting was made on the Refuge in 2000 and an increasing number of sightings are occurring north of the Refuge, but no official data is available.

The yellow mud turtle is another Refuge species of special interest and will be treated as a listed species for planning purposes. The Refuge population is centered at Gimlet Lake and is estimated at 4,000 to 5,000. A study by Earlham College, which includes the Refuge, provides good information on the biology of the turtle (Iverson, Annual Study Reports).

Birds

Nebraska includes 413 species on its official bird list, 279 of which occur on Crescent Lake Refuge (Appendix F).

Species of Special Interest. For the purposes of this plan, Wildlife Species of Management Concern are those listed by the U.S. Fish & Wildlife Service, the State of Nebraska, or Partners in Flight as declining and in need of special attention. Comparing these lists with the Refuge bird list indicates 25 such species occur on the Refuge sometime during the year (Appendix H). Little is known about the status and trends of most of these birds or how they are affected, positively or negatively, by present habitat management.

Waterfowl. Thirty-two species use the Refuge during some portion of the year and 15 species nest on the Refuge. Peak numbers during the fall migration occur in October and averaged 13,100 over the last 10 years. Peak numbers during the spring migration occur in April and averaged 12,600 over the same period. Table 1 shows average peak numbers by species.

Figure 2. Average Peak Waterfowl Populations by Species During Fall Migration, 1985-95 (*Nests on the Refuge)

Species	Average Peak No.
* Trumpeter swan	29
* Canada goose	1,050
* Mallard	4,860
* Gadwall	4,960
* Pintail	1,370
* Green-winged teal	1,400
* Blue-winged teal	730
* Cinnamon teal	30
* Wigeon	3,075
* Shoveler	4,140
* Redhead	4,232
Ring-necked duck	4,950
* Canvasback	3,660
* Lesser Scaup	3,840
Common goldeneye	3,000
* Bufflehead	5,520
* Ruddy duck	3,420
Common merganser	600

Although the Sandhills, as a whole, are the most important waterfowl production area in the State, Crescent Lake is not considered a waterfowl production refuge per se. Duck breeding pairs ranged from 548 to 1,450 since 1987, a period which included very dry and very wet years on both the Refuge and on portions of the major breeding grounds to the north. The number of ducklings hatched ranged from 1,000 to 3,500. Among dabbling ducks, blue-winged teal are the most common nesters (62 percent), followed by mallards (33 percent), gadwalls (3 percent), pintails (1 percent), and shovelers (1 percent). For diving ducks, ruddy ducks are the most common nesters (48 percent), followed by redheads (43 percent) and canvasbacks (9 percent).

Predation on duck nests is a limiting factor. Bullsnakes, weasels, raccoons, and skunks are the major predators. Without predator control, nest success rates hover around 16 percent, the bottom end of the rate needed for population maintenance. An intensive bullsnake removal program during the 1980s resulted in nest success rates up to 50 percent on a small sample area. However, because nest densities are relatively low, the resulting small increase in numbers of ducks produced to flight stage could not be justified, and the program was discontinued in 1994. Extensive predator control has not occurred on the Refuge since then.

There are 98 Canada goose nesting tubs on the Refuge, about 60 percent of which are used annually. Hatching success is around 80 percent and between 200 and 250 goslings are raised to flight stage. Few geese nest off the artificial structures.

Marsh and Water Birds. Eared grebes nest on Goose and Deer Lakes. Numbers vary considerably from year-to-year, and during the last 10 years ranged from 446 adults and 290 nests to 1,194 adults and 656 nests.

There is a long-standing double-crested cormorant rookery on Goose Lake, and cormorants pioneered onto Crane Lake in 1997. The number of nests over the last 10 years averaged about 60.

Great blue herons nest in the Crane Lake rookery. The number of nests in the last 4 years ranged from 43 to 127; production estimates range from 94 to 125 young hatched.

Black-crowned night-herons have traditionally nested at Smith Lake but, for unknown reasons, the colony moved to Goose Lake in 1997. The number of nests in the last 10 years ranged from 3 to 11.

American bitterns were first surveyed in 1996 (a breeding male song survey on Smith, Goose, Gimlet and Island Lakes). From 1996 to 1999, the number of males ranged from 24 to 35.

A rail call survey was initiated in 1997 and yields only trend information. Virginia rail calls went from 36 to 20 and sora rail calls from 6 to zero in the period 1997 to 1999.

Shorebirds, Gulls, Terns, and Allied Species. Thirty-one shorebird species, 7 gull species, and 5 tern species occur on the Refuge. Of these, 11 species nest on the Refuge (Appendix F). No formal surveys are conducted. Peak numbers of all species seldom exceed 2,500 in spring and 1,000 in fall.

Raptors. The open grasslands of the Sandhills, interspersed with small areas of trees, provide excellent habitat and food sources for raptors. Twenty-seven species have been recorded on the Refuge. Figure 3 presents 1997 breeding survey results, an average year.

Figure 3. 1997-1999 Raptor Breeding Survey Results

Species	Average Breeding Pairs	Average No. Young
Red-tailed hawk	2	4 (est.)
Swainson's hawk	5	8
Bald eagle	1	2
Great horned owl	2	3
Northern harrier	8	Unknown
American kestrel	4	15
Barn owl (in nest structures)	8	24

Non-migratory Birds. Prairie grouse, a significant component of the Nebraska Sandhills, are declining throughout their range (Proceedings Prairie Grouse Technical Conference 1998). Crescent Lake Refuge is also seeing declines. Sharp-tailed grouse lek surveys from 1986 to 1997 show active dancing grounds decreasing from 45 to 15 and dancing males decreasing from 413 to 109. Refuge populations seemed to rebound in 1998 and 1999 when the number of dancing grounds averaged 32 and the number of dancing males averaged 226. The causes for the decline and the significance of the recent increases are not clear.

The Refuge is on the western edge of the range of the greater prairie chicken. This species has not been present with regularity since the 1950s, and then numbers seldom exceeded 100. Reintroduction projects in the 1970s and 1980s were unsuccessful. A single male was seen on the Refuge in the spring of 2000, and five were heard during the lek counts.

Ring-necked pheasants, exotic but popular game birds, occur in relatively small numbers. The average breeding population from 1987 to 1999 was 361.

Mammals

The Sandhills provide habitat for a variety mammals (Appendix F). Pre-settlement mammalian fauna included 59 species. Ten carnivores and ungulates were probably extirpated by 1900, including the bison, elk, and bighorn sheep. Ten mammals have been introduced or their natural ranges extended, including the fox squirrel, black-tailed jackrabbit, and raccoon (Jones 1964).

White-tailed deer and mule deer are both present. The best populations estimates are from the period 1979 to 1991 when aerial surveys were conducted. Estimated average populations during that period were 110 mule deer and 152 white-tailed deer. Populations have not significantly changed since that period, although aerial surveys are cost-prohibitive and were replaced with less accurate ground surveys. The largest harvests since the hunter check station was initiated in 1981 occurred in 1998 and 1999 when 66 and 47 deer were checked respectively. The average harvest since 1981 is 32.

Because of their economic importance and because they can alter wetland habitat, muskrats have been surveyed by counting houses in the winter since the Refuge was established. Population peaks occurred in 1950 (934 houses), 1989 (1,929 houses), and 1996 (742 houses). During the last peak, considerable opening of cattail marshes was noted.

Coyote scat counts were initiated in 1997 and supply population trends which have been stable during the survey period. Estimates of population numbers are not available.

There is no data for population trends of other mammal species.

Amphibians and Reptiles

The most common reptiles and amphibians are tiger salamander, northern prairie lizard, bullsnake, garter snake, and box turtle (Appendix F). The yellow mud turtle is considered a Refuge species of special interest and is discussed under endangered species.

Fish

Fisheries have been managed by the NGPC under an agreement with the Refuge since 1991, when FWS fisheries capabilities were reduced. Island Lake has been open to sport fishing since 1931. Carp were eliminated in 1978, and the lake now supports warm water species including largemouth bass, bluegill, crappie, yellow perch, walleye, and sauger. However, a few carp of even-age class were discovered in the spring of 2000 and the problem may reemerge.

Carp were reduced, but not eliminated, in Smith Lake in 1996. That lake now supports a perch/panfish fishery but may develop a serious carp problem in the future. Crane Lake is the only other lake with sport fishery potential and was stocked with yellow perch in 2000. The fathead minnow, the only other fish species on the Refuge, was introduced into several lakes in the late 1970s. The minnow provides a food source for a variety of birds but also creates turbid water, an undesirable result.

Cultural Resources

Little formal archaeological work has been conducted within the Nebraska Sandhills. Collections by avocational archaeologists indicate the area has a long prehistoric record and that artifacts are widely distributed; however, because of the unique nature of the Sandhills, settlement and subsistence patterns are difficult to predict (Burgett and Nickel 1999). No systematic surveys have been conducted on the Refuge, and no known Native American sites exist.

Historic use of the Sandhills is better documented. Only a few fur trade and ranching operations existed prior to the Federal government's decision to survey the region and make it available for homesteading in 1904. Nearly all early attempts at farming failed and homesteads were aggregated into efficient and successful ranching operations. No farm or ranch buildings remain on the Refuge but old dump sites are still scattered across the area. Two Refuge buildings and two fire towers built by the CCC and WPA in the 1930s are subject to conditions of Federal laws protecting historic resources.

Public Use

Crescent Lake offers a variety of public use opportunities including hunting, fishing, wildlife viewing, photography, hiking, and environmental education (Map 5). Public trapping has been allowed on a permit basis. About 7,000 to 9,000 people visited Crescent Lake in recent years, a drop of over 30 percent from the 13,000 recorded in 1987. Counting methods varied somewhat throughout the period and may be the reason for this drop.

Most visitors engage in more than one activity but the primary reason for visits in recent years can be categorized as follows:

Hunting	3%
Fishing	67%
Wildlife viewing and photography	28%
Education/Interpretation	2%

The Refuge is open to hunting for mule and white-tailed deer, prairie grouse, and ring-necked pheasants. It is not open for waterfowl, other migratory birds, or predators, such as coyotes. The 5-year average for deer hunting is 200 visits; the average for upland game is 300 visits. Some hunters hunt for both deer and upland game during the same visit.

Fishing on Island and Smith Lakes is the most popular use of the Refuge. In recent years, fishing visits averaged about 5,000, of which 20 percent occurred during winter months. Supporting facilities are limited to two graveled boat ramps and two fishing piers on Island Lake. Boats are only allowed on Island Lake and gas powered engines are prohibited.
Formal education/interpretation facilities are limited to one auto tour route along the County road and modest information kiosks and displays at the headquarters. The Refuge is available as an outdoor classroom; however, the isolated location, sparse local population, and distances to schools limits use to about 200 students per year.

IV. Refuge Goals, Objectives, and Strategies

Background

This is a 15-year plan, but only the goals will remain static. Objectives and strategies are based on present knowledge and reflect known needs. They may change, as may specific management actions, as knowledge and needs change. Public involvement will be sought for any significant amendments.

It is also important to understand that individual objectives cannot be taken out of context. It is the mixture of objectives that will produce the desired results. Generally speaking, on Crescent Lake Refuge, where the legal mandate is to serve as a "refuge and breeding ground for birds and other wild animals," habitat is managed to support or produce birds and other wildlife. However, because it is the habitat over which wildlife managers have most control, a clear understanding must also occur of the kinds and amounts of habitat needed to support that wildlife. Public use and environmental education are also important functions of the Refuge. Thus, it is important to know what kinds and how much public use can be allowed and remain compatible with the wildlife purposes and objectives.

Although ecological diversity is part of the Refuge vision, the Refuge is limited in size and cannot be all things to all forms of wildlife. Therefore, in order to decide how much of specific habitats are needed and how to manage those habitats, it is necessary to define which animals or groups of animals will receive priority and where. For instance, if a conflict exists between providing for a species listed as 'threatened" under the Endangered Species Act and providing for mallard ducks, the threatened species and its habitat may be given priority. Similarly, a species once part of, but now missing from, the "refuge ecosystem" may be given priority over a non-indigenous species or a species common on and off the refuge. Once such decisions are made, the types and management of habitat can be described.

The wildlife priorities for Crescent Lake Refuge are:
1. endangered or threatened species;
2. species considered candidates for listing as threatened or endangered, and Species of Management Concern (species which, based on scientific evidence, are or are becoming rare, or are steadily declining in numbers, and for which proper habitat occurs on the Refuge);
3. migratory birds;
4. species that are dependent upon some special quality of the habitat found on the Refuge;
5. fish and wildlife that people use consumptively; and
6. organisms that, because of a unique quality, are of special interest to people.

Endangered, Threatened, and Candidate Species

Plants and animals listed as endangered or threatened by either the Federal government or the State of Nebraska will receive priority in all Refuge management decisions. Only two are known to use the Refuge in any significant way (See Section III, Refuge and Resource Descriptions). The federally-listed blowout penstemon, a plant which grows only on sand soils in areas devoid of other vegetation; and the State-listed swift fox. The Refuge is in the heart of the remaining penstemon habitat. The swift fox is an infrequent and casual visitor but an increasing number of sightings are being recorded in the vicinity, primarily just off the Refuge to the north. A third species, the yellow mud turtle, is a sensitive species and, as such, will also receive priority consideration.

Goal 1: *Contribute to the preservation and restoration of endangered flora and fauna that are or were endemic to the Crescent Lake Refuge area.*

Objective: Maintain five population groups of blowout penstemon with at least 300 plants in each group (one half of the Recovery Plan goal).

Native plants declined from 2,050 in the first survey in 1987 to 608 in 1996 (see Figure 1). A transplant program was started in 1997 in cooperation with the University of Nebraska. The penstemon survey conducted in 2000 found 1,032 plants (not including plants transplanted that spring). Although the number of plants on the Refuge has increased, the survival rate of the transplants is low and the immediate future seems to include a continuous input of hand-grown plants. It also appears that habitat shrinkage is not the only reason for declining numbers. There are many blowouts with suitable habitat where the plants continue to decline. A large number of new blowouts were started in the winter of 1997 but none were colonized by 1999. Transplants appear more vigorous and it may be that native plants have become genetically deficient from many years of isolation. Transplantation may result in increased vigor over time.

Strategies:
- Continue the transplant program; monitor population status, survival rates, colonization, and other parameters to evaluate and adjust management.
- Prepare maps showing the past, present, and desired location of penstemon populations on and nearby the Refuge, and overlay information regarding numbers of plants, densities, transplants, etc.
- Protect existing penstemon populations on private lands adjacent to the Refuge.

Blowout penstemon, University of Nebraska

Objective: Attempt to verify swift fox use on the Refuge.

The Refuge is not considered prime swift fox habitat and the fox is a casual visitor. Their primary range is west of the Refuge.

Strategies:
- Investigate sightings and use scent stations to aid in verifying presence of swift fox.
- Conduct literature search to find ways that habitat may be enhanced for swift fox.

Objective: Maintain present population numbers of 4,000 to 5,000 yellow mud turtles and protect their habitat.

The yellow mud turtle is a Species of Management Concern due to low numbers and isolated populations. It is found in only five small areas in the Nebraska Sandhills. The remainder of the turtle's range extends from southern Nebraska through Texas and into Mexico. On the Refuge, it is found almost exclusively at Gimlet Lake. A second large population occurs at Rush Lake, just off the Refuge. Refuge population estimates range from 3,000 to 4,000. These turtles migrate across the County road twice a year and are especially vulnerable to road kill and predation at those times. Improvements in the County road along Gimlet Lake could result in increased mortality from vehicles due to more traffic and higher speeds. A long-term study by Dr. John Iverson of Earlham College, Richmond, Indiana, has provided valuable information regarding the biology of the turtle; however, information is limited that provides specific guidance for preservation and management of this species.

Strategies:
- Continue to support the studies conducted by Earlham College and seek information leading to specific management actions.
- Seek ways to eliminate mortality on the County road during migrations.
- Consider yellow mud turtles in all habitat management decisions for Gimlet Lake and their nesting and hibernating area north and east of Gimlet lake during development of the Habitat Management Plan.

Special Places
Wilderness

The Wilderness Act of 1964 (Public Law 88-577/16 U.S.C. 1131-1136) defines wilderness as:

"A wilderness, in contrast with those areas where man and his works dominate the landscape, is hereby recognized as an area where the earth and its community of life are untrammeled by man, where man himself is a visitor who does not remain. An area of wilderness is further defined to mean in this Act an area of undeveloped Federal land retaining its primeval character and influence, without permanent improvements or human habitation, which is protected and managed so as to preserve its natural conditions and which (1) generally appears to have been affected primarily by the forces of nature, with the imprint of man's work substantially unnoticeable; (2) has outstanding opportunities for solitude or a primitive and unconfined type of recreation; (3) has at least 5,000 acres of land or is of sufficient size to make practicable its preservation and use in an unimpaired condition; and (4) may also contain ecological, geological, or other features of scientific, educational, scenic, or historical value."

In 1972, 24,502 acres of the Refuge were proposed for inclusion in the National Wilderness Preservation System (see Map 2). Congress has not acted on that proposal. In the intervening years, the area has been managed to maintain and improve the wilderness characteristics that existed at the time of the proposal. For instance, in 1972, there were 42 miles of fence, 39 windmills, and 44 miles of two-track trails within the area. Today, there are 34 miles of fence and 30 windmills; and the two-track trails have been closed and many have healed over.

Goal 2: Maintain and restore the wilderness qualities of the Proposed Wilderness Area.

One of the objectives for the Refuge is to reintroduce bison into the Poposed Wilderness (see Fish and Wildlife Objectives). To do that will require preparation of a bison management plan and a significant increase in funding and staff; a process that could take years. In the interim, the wildlife and habitat management objectives presented in this Plan will apply to the proposed wilderness but the management practices and tools used to implement those objectives will be "minimized." For instance, motorized vehicles will be used to access the area for noxious weed control only when no other feasible alternatives exist and the action is essential to maintain the grassland ecosystem (see Appendix G).

A need exists for a grazing animal within the Proposed Wilderness because prolonged rest will result in habitat degradation. Cattle have been used for that purpose in the past. On the Refuge, bison (if approved for reintroduction) would be free ranging and present seasonally or, perhaps, year-round; they would become part of the landscape. Their presence may change the appearance of habitats within the wilderness but in ways that would make it more like the Sandhills Prairie that existed pre-development. In fact, bison tend to create blowouts that would be beneficial to the endangered blowout penstemon.

The specific impacts of bison will be analyzed and presented in a bison management plan. While bison would add to the natural diversity of the Proposed Wilderness, they would be reintroduced only if compatible with the other wilderness purposes.

Interim Objectives (without the presence of bison):
All wildlife and habitat management objectives in this Plan would apply to the Proposed Wilderness until the decision whether or not to reintroduce bison is made.

Interim Strategies (without the presence of bison):
- Prepare, by May 1, 2003, an interim wilderness management plan that reevaluates the use of cattle grazing and fire to maintain wilderness characteristics, and further defines the use of "minimum tools." This Plan would be rewritten to reflect the presence of bison, should that event occur.

    The present Upland Habitat Management Plan calls for cattle grazing on a 20-year rotation on sands and choppy sands range sites, and a 6-year rotation on the meadows. Prescribed burning could possibly be substituted for cattle in the meadows. The minimum use of other tools must be more clearly defined, especially the use of motorized access for noxious weed control, law enforcement, wildfire control, management for blowout penstemon (an endangered species), and facilities maintenance. Public use must also be reevaluated. See Appendix G for a preliminary discussion of "minimum tools" and how they might be applied.
- Continue to remove all permanent fences and other livestock facilities not essential to maintain the prairie ecosystem.
- Establish monitoring systems to: evaluate the effects of "minimum" management on wilderness characteristics (to be defined in the interim wilderness management plan); and compare habitat and wildlife use in the wilderness with surrounding Refuge and private lands.
- Seek from the NGPC concurrence for a special regulation which will allow hunters to bone out deer in the field within the proposed wilderness.

Research Natural Areas

Two Research Natural Areas were established in 1955 by a Director's Order and included on a National list of Research Areas (see Map 2). The Goose Lake RNA is 904 acres and the Hackberry RNA is 172 acres. The purposes of Research Natural Areas are: (1) to preserve examples of undisturbed ecosystems for comparison with those influenced by man; (2) to provide educational and research areas for scientists to study ecology, successional trends, and other aspects of the natural environment; and (3) to serve as gene pools and preserves for rare and endangered species of plants and animals.

Both RNAs are treated as separate habitat units in the Upland Management Plan (1996). These areas have been allowed to evolve without interference. Habitat manipulation has been essentially non-existent. Neither area has been grazed since 1955. A portion of the meadow along Goose Lake was included in a prescribed burn in 1985. No wildfires have occurred. Noxious weeds have been controlled since 1992 when Canada thistle invaded the meadows of both units. Both areas are within the closed area of the Refuge, and public use has not been allowed. Unfortunately, no significant research has occurred in either area in part because of the remoteness of the Refuge. See the Upland Habitat Plan for additional information.

Goal 3: Preserve plant and animal communities in a natural state for research purposes.

Objective: Maintain 1,076 acres of the Research Natural Area in a condition approaching grassland climax stages and affected only by natural forces.

> Strategies:
> - Initiate management practices only where necessary to preserve vegetation and only when in compliance with the Natural Area Management Plan (8 RM 10.8 H).
> - Reduce total thistle acreage, and any other noxious plants that appear, using integrated pest management techniques. Eradication is not feasible but the plant should not be allowed to spread or become the dominant species in a given area.

Upland Habitat

Goal 4: Preserve, restore, and enhance the ecological diversity of indigenous flora and fauna of the physiographic region described as the Sandhills Prairie.

An Upland Habitat Management Plan was approved for Crescent Lake Refuge in 1996. Referred to as a "step-down plan," it presents specific habitat descriptions and management techniques that will enhance and maintain the required habitat necessary to sustain wildlife populations and achieve stated habitat objectives. The following objectives are taken from that document.

The general theme of grassland or prairie management on Crescent Lake Refuge is to maximize native warm season grasses and create a general landscape that resembles "native" Sandhills Prairie throughout the year. This is desirable because surrounding private lands have a different purpose (primarily cattle production) and, thus, have less residual cover available in the early spring for ground-nesting birds. Cool season and exotic grasses (such as Kentucky bluegrass, smooth brome, and cheatgrass) begin growing in early spring and reach maturity (cure out) in mid-summer. By the following spring, they are mostly lying flat and of little use to nesting birds. Native warm season grasses do not begin to grow until early or mid-summer. They are generally bigger, more robust, and remain standing throughout winter and spring. Many bird species are adaptable and can survive in less than optimum habitat, although their numbers are generally fewer. However, some species of birds have specific habitat requirements and are decreasing throughout their range or becoming rare because of changes in vegetation structure and composition resulting from commercial uses. The Refuge can and should provide habitats not common on surrounding private lands.

Five major habitat types occur on the Refuge. These include: Wetlands (open water, seasonally flooded, and emergent vegetation 3,110 acres), Subirrigated Meadows (4,195 acres), Sands (27,611 acres), Choppy Sand (1,718 acres), and Sands/Choppy Sands (8,653 acres) mix (see Map 4). These types are defined by a combination of soil type, slope, plant composition, and moisture. Goals, objectives, and strategies will be defined by habitat type. The Refuge also has two Research Natural Areas and a Proposed Wilderness Area requiring special management strategies to achieve habitat and wildlife goals and objectives.

The following objectives are designed to result in a landscape simulating native prairie habitat which will support a diversity of wildlife species. These objectives apply to the entire Refuge, including the Proposed Wilderness Area (see Wilderness objectives). How these objectives are achieved will be slightly different within the Proposed Wilderness Area because, there, the use of management tools must be minimized. The Wilderness Area will be managed under an interim plan until a Wilderness Management Plan is written.

Objective: Develop a vegetative map (in GIS format) that follows the Nebraska Range Site description (NRCS 1995) or is consistent with and/or is easily cross-walked to the NRCS system showing past, present, and desired structure and composition by 2005.

Strategy:
- Contract vegetative mapping to be stored in a GIS Arcview system.

Subirrigated Meadow

Goal 5: Preserve, restore, and enhance the ecological diversity of indigenous flora and fauna of the Subirrigated Meadow habitat type.

Past and present management on subirrigated meadows encouraged grass species which provide tall and dense residual cover (e.g. switch grass, Indian grass, big bluestem). Prescribed fire and spring grazing treatment using cattle were, in the past and are now, the primary tools. When the desired landscape is achieved, use of these tools will be minimized to allow maximum nest success. Nest site vegetative structure has been determined for most Species of Management Concern.

The emphasis will be placed on the following wildlife species of management concern when managing for specific vegetation composition and structure in the subirrigated meadow habitat type: eastern meadowlark, prairie chicken, upland sandpiper, Swainson's hawk, short-eared owl, loggerhead shrike, northern harrier, bobolink, and dickcissel. Wildlife species requiring the same habitat quality and type that will also benefit, but not considered species of management concern as defined by the Service, are American avocet, willet, Wilson's phalarope, bobolink, and waterfowl (primarily blue-winged teal, mallard, gadwall, pintail, and shoveler).

Duck nesting preferences are well known. Refuge nest studies indicate that upland nesting ducks generally prefer the tall, mature, dense cover of the subirrigated meadows. The literature supports this general conclusion (Duebbert 1966 and 1969; Duebbert and Lokemoen 1976; Imler 1942, unpub. data; Bue 1952; Clark 1977; Gjersing 1975; and Kirsch 1978). Upland nesting ducks on the Refuge include the blue-winged teal (62%), mallard (33%), gadwall (3%), pintail (1%), and shoveler (1%).

Although sharp-tailed grouse prefer the northeast slopes of sandhills, they do require tall residual cover and will nest in the subirrigated meadows. Prairie chickens have not nested on the Refuge since the early 1970s but, when present, relied almost totally on the subirrigated meadow type for nest and brood habitat.

Objective: Maintain 90 to 100 percent native grass composition on 4,195 acres of subirrigated habitat to meet the needs of species of management concern and associated species as outlined above. Plant composition will consist of approximately 80 to 85 percent grass and sedges (big bluestem, Indian grass, Canada wildrye, prairie cordgrass, slender wheatgrass, prairie sandreed, prairie June grass, sand bluestem, switchgrass and various sedges and rushes), 5 to 15 percent forbs, and less than 10 percent shrubs.

Strategy:
- Develop management treatments using grazing and burning in a Habitat Management Plan based on wildlife species priorities and unit floristics as outlined in the Upland Management Plan.

Objective: Increase (by 5 to 10 percent) or maintain the warm season grass component with native grass species, primarily Indian grass, prairie cordgrass, prairie sandreed, switchgrass, sand and big bluestem, and Canada wildrye, while reducing by 5 to 10 percent introduced cool season grasses, Kentucky bluegrass and reed canary grass.

Strategy:

n   Utilize spring grazing and fall disturbance (grazing, burning) to set-back cool season grasses and favor warm season grasses. (See Upland Management Plan for details on timing and stocking rates.)

Objective: Maintain and/or increase residual nesting cover in the spring by creating Visual Observation Reading (VORS) in the following categories: (primarily for shorebirds, waterfowl, bobolinks, and eastern meadow larks) <0.5 dm (~15 percent) (shorebirds), 0.5-1. dm (~ 20 percent) (shorebirds), 1-1.5 dm (~15 percent) (waterfowl), 1.5-2 dm (~15 percent) (waterfowl, eastern meadowlark, bobolink), 2-2.5 dm (~10 percent) (waterfowl), >2.5 dm at least 25 percent (northern harrier and short-eared owl). This information is based on Refuge data nest site vegetation structure collected from 1997 to 2001.

Strategies:

■   Graze, burn, or hay <u>no more</u> than 40 percent of the subirrigated meadow type in any one year.
■   Remove <u>no more</u> than 10 percent of warm season grass residual cover in fall (late September - early October).
■   Utilize spring and fall disturbance to set-back cool season grasses and favor warm season grasses.

Some passerine birds, for example western kingbird and orchard oriole, are present on the Refuge only because of the existing tree cover. Loggerhead shrikes and Swainson's hawks (both Species of Management Concern), great blue herons, and bald eagles are also dependent on trees. Unless there is a demonstrated biological need for more of any species dependent on this habitat, tree cover will be maintained at approximately present amounts and locations. Resident species such as white-tailed deer, mule deer, sharp-tailed grouse, and ring-necked pheasants are dependent, to some degree, on the few trees on the Refuge.

Objective: Maintain tree cover at the present 80 acres with emphasis on willow and cottonwood regeneration.

Strategies:

■   Mechanically remove Russian olive which have the potential for rapid expansion.
■   Protect willow and cottonwood saplings near current aging trees.

Objective: Reduce total acreage of Canada thistle infestation from the approximate 800 acres (at present) to 350 acres by 2008 and continue control measures in the future to prevent additional acreage infestation.

Strategy:

■   Manage Canada thistle using integrated pest management techniques. Eradication is not feasible but the plant should not be allowed to spread or become the dominant species in a given area. Eradicate and/or control, by mechanical removal and spot application of appropriate herbicides, other noxious plants as they appear.

Sands, Choppy Sands, and Sands/Choppy Sands Mixed Habitats

There are 3 habitat types of uplands on Crescent Lake Refuge based on NRCS habitat typing. They are Sands (27,611 acres), Sandy (which is combined with sands because there is only one small site on the Refuge), and Choppy Sands (1,718 acres). There are also areas of mixed habitat were the scale did not allow Sands and Choppy Sands to be delineated (8,653 acres). In the mixed types, there are those considered Sand/Choppy Sands Mix > 60 percent, Sands and Choppy Sands/Sands Mix > 60 percent, and Choppy Sands. Based on vegetation, structure and species composition these areas need to be separated for management purposes to meet specific wildlife goals.

Goal 6: Preserve, restore, and enhance the ecological diversity of indigenous flora and fauna of the Sands, Choppy Sands, and Sands/Choppy Sands Mixed habitat types.

Undeveloped Sandhill Prairie supported a mixture of tall warm season grasses, shorter cool season grasses, and a variety of forbs. Today, this native mixture is not common on surrounding private rangeland. However, these private lands do provide an abundance of short grasses for wildlife which need short grass for all or a part of their life cycle. While the original mosaic cannot be duplicated, by emphasizing warm season grasses and forbs on the Refuge, a mixture of habitats can be provided over a larger area.

Species which will benefit from taller vegetation include the grasshopper sparrow, bobolink, and prairie chicken. Birds which may be disposed to shorter grass surrounding the Refuge include killdeer, willet, horned lark, and lark bunting (Kantrud 1982; Kirsch 1978; and Ryder 1980).

The year-round requirements of sharp-tailed grouse are met by the mixture of grasses and forbs on the sands and choppy sands range sites. They do show a preference for the northeast slopes of sandhills for nesting, often adjacent to subirrigated meadows, although they will also nest in the meadows.

Duebbert (1974) states "Residual nesting cover or dead vegetation carried over from year-to-year is a very important component of nesting cover. However, if the non-use period extends for too many years, the vigor of the vegetation and its value as nesting cover eventually declines. A system of vegetative management that includes several years of non-use interrupted by nearly complete cover removal during one year appears to maintain good nesting."

The desired vegetation and wildlife use on these two range sites is encouraged by a combination of fire, grazing, and rest. Management will strive for a balance between providing undisturbed wildlife cover and maintaining vegetative composition and structure to benefit primarily grasshopper sparrows, western meadowlarks, sharp-tailed grouse, mourning doves, vesper sparrows, and lark sparrows.

Objective: Maintain 90 to 100 percent native grass composition on Sands (27,611 acres), Choppy Sands (1,718 acres), and Sands/Choppy sands (8,653 acres) mixed habitat types to meet the needs of species of management concern and associated species as outlined above. Plant composition will consist of approximately 80 to 85 percent grass and sedges; (blue and hairy grama grass, sand lovegrass, needle-and-thread, sand dropseed, prairie sandreed, prairie June grass, sand bluestem, switchgrass) and 5 to 10 percent forbs.

Strategies:
- Develop management treatments using grazing and burning in a Habitat Management Plan based on wildlife species priorities and unit floristics as outlined in the Upland Management Plan.
- Implement spring grazing and fall vegetation disturbance to set-back cool season grasses and favor warm season grasses. (See current Upland Management Plan for details on timing and stocking rates.)

Objective: Increase the warm season grass component of the Sand and Choppy Sands range types by 10 percent; emphasize sand bluestem in sand range sites and sand bluestem, sand dropseed, and sand lovegrass in choppy sands range sites.

Strategies:
- Utilize spring and fall disturbance to set-back cool season grasses and favor warm season grasses. (See current Upland Management Plan for details on timing and stocking rates.)
- Conduct one prescribed burn on a Sand or Choppy Sand range site each year as a test to determine the effects of burning on habitat and wildlife use and the effects of fire on creation and maintenance of blowout penstemon habitat.
- Do not graze/burn/hay more than 40 percent of the Sands habitat type in any one year.
- Do not remove more than 10 percent of warm season grass residual cover in the fall.

Objective: Maintain quality nesting cover by providing residual cover in spring. Develop spring VORS in the 0.5-1. 5 dm (grasshopper sparrow) and 1.5-2.5 dm (upland sandpiper, long billed curlew, sharp-tailed grouse) ranges on 40 percent and 20 percent of VOR readings respectively. (Based on nest site vegetation structure data from Refuge records collected 1997-2000.)

Strategies:
- Do not graze/burn/hay more than 40 percent of the Sands, Sands/ Choppy type any one year.
- Do not remove more than 10 percent of warm season grass cover in fall (late September - early October).
- Utilize spring and fall disturbance to set-back cool season grasses and favor warm season grasses. (See current Upland Management Plan for details on timing and stocking rates.)
- Utilize inter-seeding of sand bluestem, prairie sandreed and switchgrass in pockets, to develop higher VOR areas for nesting, thermal, and escape cover.

Choppy Sands and Sands/Choppy Sands Mix

Choppy Sands site have been separated from Sands site because they provide unique habitat for Refuge species. Blowout penstemon occurs in this habitat were blowouts are more likely to occur. Lark sparrow also only nest in this habitat type on the Refuge because the habitat type meets the open requirements of this grassland nester.

Goal 7: Preserve, restore, and enhance the ecological diversity of indigenous flora and fauna of the Choppy and Sands/Choppy Sands mix habitat types.

Historically, the Sandhills had large amounts of blowouts and bare sand runs. Possibly more than 50 percent may have been open sand. Blowout penstemon was common. Historical fire intervals were 3 to 5 years, with spring and fall wildfires. Species of Management Concern and associated species include: lark sparrow, sharp-tailed grouse, mourning dove, western meadowlark, vesper sparrow, grasshopper sparrow, upland sandpiper, long-billed curlew, and blowout penstemon.

Objective: Create and maintain blowouts in five habitat units to maintain blowout penstemon populations. The Refuge currently has 180 blowouts that historically have had penstemon. They average about 10 yards in diameter; some larger, some smaller. Within the five habitat units, we found 80 penstemon plants in 2002.

Strategies:
- Reduce cover by frequent disturbance to expose sand to wind, primarily through fall grazing.
- Use mechanical means to create new blowouts in areas where blowouts have healed.
- Disturb designated areas on an average of every 3 to 4 years with some variation in time and intensity of grazing.
- Protect plants from grazing in May and early June.
- Plant seedlings provided by the University of Nebraska, Lincoln.
- Monitor the success of each action taken to verify and quantify results.

Objective: Maintain 90 to 100 percent native grass composition on Choppy Sands (1,718 acres) and Sands/Choppy Sands (8,653 acres) mix habitat types to meet the needs of Species of Management Concern and associated species as outlined above. Plant composition will consist of approximately 90 to 95 percent grass and sedges (sandhills muhly, blue and hairy grama grass, sand lovegrass, needle-and-thread, sand dropseed, blowout grass, prairie sandreed, prairie June grass, sand bluestem, switchgrass) and 5 to 10 percent forbs.

Strategies:
- Develop species priority for each habitat unit and develop grazing and burning treatments within the Habitat Management Plan based on individual unit floristics (identified in the 1996 Upland Management Plan).
- Implement spring and fall grazing and prescribe burning programs with different durations of rest, depending on units and wildlife uses, to set-back cool season grasses and stimulate warm season grasses.
- Maintain 20 to 40 percent bare ground, or less than 60 percent litter cover, using rest rotation grazing cycles every 3 to 4 years.

Objective: Maintain quality nesting cover by providing residual cover in spring. Develop spring VORS in the 0.5-1.5 dm (to meet open requirements of some species) and 1.5-2.5 dm (lark sparrow, sharp-tailed grouse) ranges on 40 percent and 20 percent of VOR readings respectively.

Strategies:
- Do not graze/burn/hay more than 40 percent of the Choppy and Sands/Choppy Sands mix types in any one year.
- Do not remove more than 10 percent of warm season grass residual cover in the fall.
- Utilize spring and fall disturbance to set-back cool season grasses and favor warm season grasses. (See current Upland Management Plan for details on timing and stocking rates.)

Wilderness - *Special considerations to above habitat goals, objectives, and strategies*

Goal 8: Preserve, restore, and enhance the ecological diversity of indigenous flora and fauna of the physiographic region described as the Sandhills Prairie, while maintaining and enhancing the wilderness quality.

Objective: Maintain the integrity of the 24,502-acre Proposed Wilderness Area as intended by Congress in the Wilderness Act of 1964, Service policy, and Director's Order #116, Wilderness Stewardship Training.

Strategy:
- Utilize bison and, where possible, prescribed fire as a "natural" disturbance to meet above habitat goals, objectives, and strategies.

The Refuge staff believes that neither the wilderness characteristics nor the established wildlife goals can be met without the use of grazing and fire.

Wetland Habitat

Wetlands (lakes and marshes) constitute about 18 percent of the total Refuge. Most wetlands are shallow and dependent on annual precipitation; only nine lakes have any potential for water level manipulation. The overriding concern is the gradual filling of wetlands by emergent vegetation, windblown sand, and decaying plant material until they eventually become dry land. This process is particularly important because the Sandhills Prairie is a managed area and becoming more stable and less subject to natural forces. Wetlands were formed during periods of prolonged drought by wind cut depressions occurring in the Sandhills landscape. As water tables were restored, wetlands appeared and vegetation stabilized the surrounding areas forming permanent wetland depressions. Wetlands are no longer being created naturally and probably will not be until the next prolonged drought, if then. Management emphasis will be placed on the following species: waterfowl, white-faced ibis, American bitterns, Virginia rails, red-winged and yellow-headed blackbirds, marsh wrens, black and Forster's terns, black-crowned night-herons, and the yellow mud turtle.

Goal 9: Maintain natural and artificially managed permanent and semipermanent wetlands to provide habitat for migratory waterfowl, shorebirds, wading birds, and associated wetland-dependent species.

Natural Lakes

There are 15 named lakes on the Refuge and more than 100 ponds of varying sizes that provide a wide range of habitats for wildlife. Each lake/wetland contains specific morphological, physiological, and biological characteristics that combine to determine the ability to support and maintain certain species of vegetation as a food source for migrating waterfowl, shorebirds, and marsh related species and as an important substrate for invertebrate resources. Natural functions are allowed to dominate these bodies of water, but can be augmented to meet specific wildlife goals or needs.

Objective: Maintain and/or augment the quality of the wetland habitat (submergent and emergent vegetation and invertebrate levels) for breeding and migrating birds as well as resident wildlife populations.

Strategies:
- Allow for a natural cycling (wet and dry cycles) to occur as a means to maintain necessary nutrient levels (e.g. plant and animal detritus) to support targeted wildlife species.
- Utilize prescribed fire and grazing on shorelines and emergent vegetation.
- Utilize pumping of lakes to eliminate the carp and allow for stabilization of lake bottoms and annual vegetation encroachment on occasion.

Objective: Prevent phragmites from occupying more than 15 percent of any wetland basin.

Strategy:
- Treat 100 percent of the phragmites areas with Rodeo (chemical treatment) where possible.

Objective: Treat other invasive wetland plants if they appear on the Refuge.

Strategy:
- Conduct annual surveys to detect the presence of any exotic wetland plant; coordinate with landowners and local County and State officials to monitor the presence or expansion of purple loosestrife on adjacent private lands.

Artificially Managed Lakes

The following lakes (wetlands) are artificially managed to provide the habitat requirements necessary for the above listed wetland-dependent species: Martin, Ramalli Marsh, Smith, Perrin, Redhead, Upper Harrison, Gimlet, West Jones, and Duck Slough. Each lake/wetland contains specific morphological, physiological, and biological characteristics that combine to determine the ability to support and maintain certain species of vegetation as a food source for migrating waterfowl, shorebirds, and marsh related species and as an important substrate for invertebrate resources. Specific resource management information and recommended management direction for these lakes and the following objectives are based on information found in Fredrickson (2001).

Water management involves water level manipulation of the lakes, limited dewatering of lakes without inflow or outflow by pumping, flowage ditches, and water control structures.

Since the 1930s, the natural lakes along the Moore Valley drainage have been equipped with water control structures and/or had small dikes constructed to increase levels and allow for manipulation of water. However, it appears that only Smith and Martin Lakes outlets were utilized prior to 1958. Also, because most of these lakes are closed drainages and permanent types of water, stagnation occurs. To remedy this, pumping for drawdown began in about 1972.

Applications for State water rights have not been filed on these lakes because Nebraska law does not allow for protection of "natural" lakes. No records exist documenting the natural elevations and the amount of additional water impounded above the natural levels.

The only Refuge water right of record is Permit No. A-16382 for 13 cfs from Eldred Lake. The lake (currently a hay meadow) is located on private lands and covered under a perpetual easement, permitting diversion of water to the Refuge via the Eldred Diversion Ditch. Consumptive water use has not be quantified.

Objective: Provide vegetative composition (sago pondweed, softstem/hardstem bulrush, spikerush, Cypersus) and structure (tall emergents) as a food source, and invertebrate substrate, for waterfowl, shorebirds, and marsh-dependent bird species during spring and fall migration and summer nesting to meet the necessary life requirements as described in the Wetland Management Plan and/or the Habitat Management Plan (to be developed).

Strategy:
- Develop a Wetland Management Plan or Habitat Management Plan incorporating the following strategies.
  - ✓ Define each lake's best wildlife use and potential and the habitat necessary to meet the life requirements needed for targeted wildlife species.
  - ✓ Utilize complete drawdowns for 1 to 2 growing seasons to recharge the nutrient cycle.
  - ✓ Utilize partial drawdowns during a single year to provide foraging habitats, with some variation in season, length, and amount of drawdown defined by wildlife needs.
  - ✓ Utilize high water levels, grazing and prescribe fire to control vegetation, with some variation in season, and length.
  - ✓ Implement complete drawdowns on <u>no more</u> than two lakes in a given year.
  - ✓ Utilize complete drawdowns and Rotenone application to eliminate carp.
  - ✓ Utilize prescribed fire and grazing on shorelines and emergent vegetation.
  - ✓ Treat cattail edges to maintain "soft" edge for waterfowl nesting.
  - ✓ Maintain the existing database of surface and groundwater resources. A record of surface and groundwater levels has been maintained almost from the establishment of the Refuge. It is essential that this record continue in order to detect vegetation and other biological changes due to changes in water levels and document wildlife use of these habitats.

Objective: Prevent phragmites from occupying more than 15 percent of any wetland basin. Phragmites are firmly established in the Refuge wetlands and are invading adjacent vegetative types. It is estimated that phragmites occupies about 2 percent of the wetland area. Total eradication is not feasible.

Strategy:
- Treat 100 percent of the phragmites areas with Rodeo (chemical treatment) where possible.

Objective: Treat other invasive wetland plants if they appear on the Refuge. Purple loosestrife, a particularly aggressive exotic plant, is found within 100 miles of the Refuge on private lands.

Strategy:
- Conduct annual surveys to detect the presence of any exotic wetland plant; coordinate with landowners and local County and State officials to monitor the presence or expansion of purple loosestrife on adjacent private lands.

Fish and Wildlife

Wildlife objectives, particularly those for migratory species, must be considered in the light of: Continental and Statewide populations and trends; the role of Crescent Lake Refuge; the potential of the Refuge to make a measurable contribution at reasonable cost; and the effect of applied management on other species. For instance, if a migratory species, or group of species, is declining because of problems on wintering grounds to the south, it does not automatically follow that this Refuge should make significant adjustments in management to produce or sustain more - but neither should that possibility be ignored. Or, for example, if increases are indicated, care should be taken that Refuge management is resulting in a net increase, not simply redistributing animals from surrounding areas.

> *"What is man without the beasts? If all the beasts were gone, men would die from a great loneliness of spirit, for whatever happens to the beasts also happens to man."*
>
> - Sealth, American Indian

Goal 10: *Preserve, restore, and enhance the ecological diversity and abundance of migratory birds and other indigenous fish and wildlife with emphasis on grassland-dependent species.*

Waterfowl

Objective: Strive to maintain a 10-year average of 15 to 20 percent Mayfield nest success in the subirrigated meadow (4,195 acres) habitat type.

Historically, between 1,000 and 3,500 ducks are hatched per year, and 80 to 100 resident Canada geese nests result in 175 to 250 goslings hatched per year. As stated before, Crescent Lake Refuge is not considered a waterfowl production refuge. The Refuge's overall contribution to the recruitment of waterfowl to the Central Flyway is considered minimal. Heavy predation by bullsnakes, weasels, coyote, skunks, and raccoons limit production of the waterfowl and, it is assumed, other upland nesting species. In the past, extraordinary efforts, such as snake fences and traps which were tended every day during the nesting season, resulted in significant increases in duck production. A 7-year average of 34.7 percent Mayfield hatch success was observed within a snake exclosure as opposed to 17.9 percent during the same period outside the exclosure. However, the effort required to maintain the fence was extraordinary and non-target species were being killed and injured in the fences. Such effort is questionable, especially when duck populations are at high levels throughout the Flyway.

Strategies:
- Achieve and maintain an interspersion and diversity of successional grassland stages as outlined in the Upland Habitat section.
- Utilize grazing (intensity, season, and duration) and prescribed burning as management tools to achieve the habitat objectives as outlined in the Upland Habitat section.

Objective: Provide nesting and brood-rearing habitat, primarily in the artificially managed lakes/wetlands, for over-water nesting ducks (redhead, canvasback, and ruddy).

Strategy:
- Develop and implement a long-term Wetland Management Plan, with goals, objectives, and strategies from Wetland section of this Plan.

Ruddy duck © Cindie Brunner

Objective: Provide quality feeding areas (abundant aquatic seed and invertebrate production), on 5 to 7 lakes where water control is possible, for spring and fall migrating waterfowl.

Strategies:
- Develop and implement a long-term Wetland Management Plan, with goals, objectives, and strategies from Wetland section, to provide quality feeding habitat.
- Provide spring feeding areas from late March through mid-May.
- Provide fall feeding areas from late August through early November.

Ground-nesting Grassland Passerines, Owls, Harriers, and Shorebirds

Of the 15 common ground-nesting passerines, owls, harriers, and shorebirds on the Refuge, nine are USFWS Region 6 Species of Management Concern. Loss or alteration of large expanses of grassland has made these species vulnerable.

Objective: Maintain and enhance breeding populations of ground-nesting grassland passerines, by achieving apparent nest success of at least 40 percent and/or the following average singing males/station: Choppy Sands and Sands/Choppy Sands mix sites - lark sparrow (2-2.5), grasshopper sparrow (0.5-1), Sands sites - grasshopper sparrow (7-9), long-billed curlew (0.1-0.5), upland sandpiper (0.1-0.5), Subirrigated Meadow sites - eastern meadowlark (1-1.5), bobolink (0.1-0.5), upland sandpiper (0.1-0.5), dickcissel (0.25-0.5).

Less work has been done with these species than the water-dependent species, but it is known that some, such as the long-billed curlew, prefer the shorter grass on the more heavily grazed areas which are common outside the Refuge (Bicak 1977; staff observations). Therefore, management designed specifically to increase such species on the Refuge may not be necessary.

However, some species are more dependent on the habitats on the Refuge. For example, a study of upland sandpiper preferences in the area of the Refuge indicated that undisturbed cover was preferred for breeding territories (Bandy 1980). Similarly, a study of habitat selection by grasshopper sparrows in Garden County Nebraska (Hopton 1996) indicated that ungrazed habitat had significantly higher populations. Therefore, more information is needed to determine how habitat management helps or hinders each species of concern and whether the Refuge has significant potential to produce or support more.

Strategies:
- Implement goals, objectives, and strategies from Upland Habitat section to provide quality breeding, nesting, and fledgling habitat.
- Devise and implement monitoring techniques to determine status, trends and effects of management on land-based Species of Management Concern.
- Increase emphasis on and knowledge of non-waterfowl species; devise and implement additional surveys and monitoring to determine population status/trends and effects of management on all Species of Management Concern.
- Develop a species richness/diversity index to establish baseline levels and measure population trends; this would apply to wildlife in general.

Objective: Provide quality feeding areas (abundant aquatic seed and invertebrate production), of exposed mud flats on 1 to 3 lakes a year where water control is possible, for spring and fall migrating shorebirds.

Strategy:
- Develop and implement a long-term Wetland Management Plan, with goals, objectives, and strategies from Wetland section of this Plan to provide quality feeding habitat.
- Provide spring feeding areas from late April through early June.
- Provide fall feeding areas from late August through early October.

Objective: Maintain breeding populations of 8 to 10 pairs of northern harriers and provide habitat for 2 to 3 pairs of short-eared owls.

Strategy:
- Implement goals, objectives, and strategies from Upland Habitat section to provide quality breeding, nesting, and fledgling habitat.

Short-eared owl © Cindie Brunner

Marsh Birds and Terns

Objective: Maintain present breeding populations and production of indigenous, water-dependent Region 6 Species of Management Concern including: American bittern, white-faced ibis, black rail, and black terns.

Objective: Maintain the habitat for nesting black and Forester's terns at Martin, Smith, Shafer, and Deer Lakes.

Objective: Maintain the habitat for nesting colonies of black-crowned night-heron and white-faced ibis on Smith and Goose lakes.

Objective: Maintain breeding populations of American bittern (.5-1), Virginia rail (.75-1.5), red-winged blackbird (3.5-5), yellow-headed blackbird (1-3), and marsh wren (2-4) based on average singing males found on the Refuge 30 station Call/Playback Survey.

American Bittern © Cindie Brunner

Strategy:
■ The above objectives will be addressed by developing and implementing a long-term Wetland Management Plan and incorporating the habitat goals, objectives, and strategies from wetland section of the CCP.

Objective: Maintain a great blue heron rookery with a target of 50 to 60 nests on Island and Crane lakes.

Strategy:
■ Maintain tree groves at Island and Crane lakes by protecting existing trees from fire and grazing and preserving natural regeneration.

Tree Nesting Species of Management Concern

Objective: Maintain habitat for a nesting population of 3 to 5 pairs of Swainson's hawk and the loggerhead shrike. Both the Swainson's hawk and loggerhead shrike are USFWS Region 6 Species of Management Concern. Their preferred habitat is large expanses of grass for feeding with occasional trees for nesting.

Strategy:
■ Maintain isolated trees throughout the Refuge by planting individual trees near current trees as replacements.

Prairie Grouse

Objective: Establish and sustain two leks of prairie chickens (8 to 12 dancing males) on the Refuge.

The prairie chicken is now a rare nester on Crescent Lake Refuge and a Refuge Species of Special Interest. The Refuge is on the edge of historical prairie chicken range, and Refuge records indicate that numbers never exceeded 100. A "trap-and-release" program conducted from 1984 to 1986 moved 275 birds onto the Refuge; all had disappeared by 1989. During the 2000 prairie grouse lek survey, a lek of 5 to 10 males was confirmed within 1/4 mile of the east boundary near Big Soddy.

In the past, prairie chickens on the Refuge used primarily subirrigated meadows for nest and brood habitat. The literature indicates that residual cover is particularly important (Kirsch 1973; Schwartz 1945; Jones 1963; Yeatter 1963; Christisen 1969; Lehman 1963; and Vichmeyer 1941). It also appears that the best prairie chicken habitat is vegetation in an early successional, sub-climax stage; this is supported by an apparent close relationship between prairie chicken success and the frequency of fire.

Although nesting requirements for prairie chickens are similar to those of some ducks (see Upland Habitat Objectives), more consideration must be given to seasonal feeding requirements, roosting habitat, and the use of management tools. Kirsch and Kruse (1973) found an increase in fruit and seed production and plant variety on burned areas. It is possible that annual requirements for prairie chickens cannot be met on the Refuge without substantial changes in upland habitat management which may or may not be compatible with management for other species. It is also possible that special management areas would have to be set up to sustain nesting populations.

    Strategies:
- By June 2003, determine the feasibility of reestablishing prairie chickens.
- If determined feasible, transplant prairie chickens at potential sites in Red Kate and Lower East Jones meadows.
- Develop and/or amend the Habitat Management Plan to reflect the goals, objectives, and strategies in the Habitat section of this Plan.

Prairie Chicken © Cindie Brunner

Objective: Maintain or enhance sharp-tailed grouse densities at a 10-year average of 220 to 250 males on dancing grounds.

In 1998, the Refuge population was 235 dancing males, significantly lower than the average of 380 in the late 1980s. An analysis of State survey data indicates that a similar decline occurred throughout western Nebraska, so the decline is not Refuge-specific. Although, specific causes of the general decline are unknown, prolonged bad weather during the nesting season and a high period in the cycle for predator populations are possibilities.

Strategies:
- Conduct an annual lek survey to determine population trends.
- Develop and augment the Habitat Management Plan to reflect goals, objectives, and strategies in the Habitat section of this Plan.
- Participate with the State in area-wide management strategies.

Objective: Strive to achieve a harvest ratio equal to or greater than 2.0 juveniles per adult based on the Refuge average harvest during stable and growing population periods.

Strategies:
- Obtain funding for a study on nest and brood rearing success.
- Develop and augment the Habitat Management Plan to reflect goals, objectives, and strategies in the Habitat section of this Plan.

Objective: Provide habitat for representative numbers of other migratory birds.

As stated earlier, species or groups of species are given some relative priorities. Migratory species that have not been identified as having some management concern are lower priority in the act of balancing the habitat for the greatest diversity. The Refuge lacks information to determine if management for higher priority species is to the detriment of others.

Strategy:
- Develop specific methods for monitoring population trends and determining the effects of habitat management on individual species or groups of species.

White-tailed deer © Cindie Brunner

Mammals, Reptiles, Amphibians, Invertebrates, and Fish

Deer

Objective: Maintain healthy deer population (300 to 400) through habitat management, population monitoring, and, if needed, harvest regulation at the Refuge level.

Deer are an important attraction because most private lands in the Sandhills are closed to public entry. Therefore, the Refuge should provide viewing opportunities. Providing such management is compatible with the needs of Federal trust species.

Both mule deer and white-tailed deer are very mobile and move on and off the Refuge. Thus, Refuge populations vary from year-to-year and season-to-season. Mule deer with identifiable characteristics often seen on the Refuge have also been seen 15 miles southwest of the Refuge. Harvest surveys have been conducted for years, however, by themselves, yield questionable results. Available information suggests that the population is not being over exploited because a substantial number of older deer are being harvested.

Strategies:
- Evaluate the reliability and usefulness of present surveys.
- Develop and augment the Habitat Management Plan to reflect goals, objectives, and strategies in the Habitat section of this Plan.
- Cooperate with the State in area-wide management strategies and annual evaluations of Refuge hunting regulations.

Mammals, Reptiles, Amphibians, and Invertebrates

Objective: Ensure the diversity and abundance of indigenous mammals, reptiles, amphibians, and invertebrate populations remain intact through habitat manipulation.

Little is known about the status and trends of these other species; thus, problems and needs may simply be unknown. Scientifically based, defendable surveys and research are very time consuming and often expensive, and past and present funding has limited such activity. Caution must be exercised because poorly designed, erratic surveys can yield misleading information. Crescent Lake Refuge is in a remote location and it is difficult to attract long-term research or volunteers on a sustainable basis.

Strategies:
- Continue to seek more information on habitat requirements and effects of management on reptiles, amphibians, fish, invertebrates, and mammals.
- Develop and augment the Habitat Management Plan to reflect goals, objectives, and strategies in the Upland and Wetland Habitat sections of this Plan.
- Establish average densities of key indicator species to document baseline levels and determine population trends.
- Continue to seek alternative ways to obtain missing information using valid, scientific methods (e.g., university studies, graduate level research, volunteer assistance for surveys and census).
- Seek funding for a permanent, full-time biologist and seasonal support staff.

Fish

Objective: Maintain fish populations to provide a food source for fish eating bird species and sport fisheries, when deemed compatible.

The Nebraska Game and Parks Commission manages sport fisheries on the Refuge with the concurrence of the refuge manager, an arrangement that has been valuable to both agencies. At present, Island, Smith, Crane, and Blue Lakes have sport fisheries. Island, Crane, and Smith Lakes have a variety of warm water species and are open to fishing. Only the corner of Blue Lake is within the Refuge; the remainder is on private land and not accessible to the public.

Carp are present in several lakes connected by a ditch in the Moore Valley, West Jones Lake and in Island Lake. Populations can be controlled by periodic drawdowns in those lakes where such control exists, including the three lakes with sport fisheries.

Strategies:
- Maintain management agreements with NGPC for Refuge sport fisheries, for NGPC monitoring Refuge fish populations, and stocking recommendations with the Refuge staff making the final management decisions.
- Write and implement long-term Wetland Management Plan with goals, objectives, and strategies coming from the Wetland section of this Plan.
- Monitor carp populations and reduce and/or eliminate them though drawdowns or pumping and pesticide treatments when water quality does not support good invertebrate populations and/or submergent vegetation.
- Maintain year-round sport fishery at Island Lake. Maintain winter fishing only on Smith and Crane lakes to minimize disturbance to wildlife.
- Evaluate any restocking of Smith Lake when carp control is needed.
- Evaluate any restocking of Crane Lake when the lake winter-kills. Crane Lake historically has experienced winter-kills about every 4 to 5 years.
- Have NGPC continue to sample and monitor Island Lake for increases in the carp population; initiate control if necessary to protect the sport fishery.
- Conduct literature search and or studies to evaluate management and habitat needs of fish eating birds to provide for their needs.

Bison

Objective: Reintroduce bison into the 24,502-acre Proposed Wilderness Area as part of an ecosystem that mimics the prairie ecosystem as it functioned before changes brought on by development.

Grazing and fire were the major factors, together with soil and climate, that interacted to make the Sandhill prairies what they were before commercial grazing and other development arrived on the scene. The grazing part of that equation was fulfilled largely by bison. Today, cattle have replaced bison and fire is infrequent and rigorously controlled.

Wilderness, on the other hand, is an idea - a concept. One envisions a "natural" area, affected only by natural forces and free from modern human influences. In the case of the proposed Crescent Lake Wilderness Area, the natural part of that vision, the wilderness characteristics themselves, cannot be maintained over time without the forces that created them in the first place. Two of those forces, fire and grazing, are now tightly controlled. A need exists for a grazing animal in the Proposed Wilderness Area and cattle, a "man-made" influence, have served that purpose in recent years - but so could bison.

The bison is the native ungulate missing from the equation. Free-ranging bison could serve as both an agent for change and an addition to biotic and aesthetic diversity. The presence of bison would contribute significantly to the legal purpose, the vision and the goals of Crescent Lake National Wildlife Refuge.

The Concept: Cattle have been used as a tool to help create and/or maintain specific grassland scenarios (see Habitat Objectives). They are allowed to graze for short periods of time under controlled conditions and only when necessary - they are not a feature of the landscape. Bison, on the other hand, would be resident wildlife, allowed to graze freely seasonally or year-round, and help simulate the natural forces with as little interference as possible. However, as fenced animals, bison would still be considered tools, and changes in numbers and grazing patterns may be needed to maintain healthy grasslands and wilderness characteristics. The emphasis would be on the wilderness ecosystem, not the bison. The presence and management of bison must also be compatible with other Wilderness and Refuge purposes.

Dale Henry

It is not the purpose of the draft CCP to present a specific proposal or to answer the many questions. It is, rather, to obtain public reaction to the concept of reintroducing bison as a natural component of a grassland ecosystem, raise the important issues and questions, and seek ideas for input into the bison management planning process.

Strategy:
■ Plan, start small, watch, learn as you go, change.

Step 1. Establish an advisory council of experienced bison and wilderness managers and wildlife biologists.

Step 2. Conduct a feasibility study and prepare a bison management plan which includes methods to: evaluate the effects of bison on the natural ecosystem, habitat and other wildlife; and compare habitat and wildlife use in the wilderness with areas outside the wilderness.

Step 3. Amend the wilderness management plan to reflect the presence and influence of bison.

Step 4. Introduce the minimum number of animals.

Step 5. Evaluate, learn, adapt, and change.

Discussion: The bison management planning process itself could take several years. If approved, it may be more years before funds and staff are available to implement the plan. In the interim, the habitat management objectives of this Plan will apply to the Proposed Wilderness Area. An interim wilderness management plan reflecting the use of minimum tools to maintain wilderness characteristics will be prepared by May 1, 2003.

The Proposed Wilderness Area is relatively small and bison cannot be present without some management. The boundary would, of course, be fenced and some interior fencing may be required. Artificial water supplies may be necessary. Overall, it is felt that bison would require less infrastructure than cattle, due to their willingness to move farther from water sources to graze. These and other issues would be addressed in the course of writing the bison management plan. There are many questions and some will be answered only through trial-and-error.

Perhaps the most important questions revolve around herd types and herd composition. There are, basically, two alternatives for the initial herd type and revolve around private herds. They are:
1. Breeding herd
2. Sterile herd

Other obvious questions are:
- How "wild" should or can this herd be?
- How will the presence of bison affect other wildlife? Habitat? Wilderness character?
- How will the presence of bison affect public use and environmental education?
- Can funding or other support be obtained through partnerships with non-government entities?

> *"But the conservation of wildness is self-defeating, for to cherish we must see and fondle, and when enough have seen and fondled, there is no wildness left to cherish."*
> — Aldo Leopold

Public Use
Interpretation and Recreation

Since Leopold made this statement, farsighted people created laws that give national wildlife refuges a protective shield called "compatibility" (see Appendix A). Public use cannot, by law, interfere with or detract from the legal purposes or the fish and wildlife objectives of a Refuge.

Crescent Lake is a rather isolated Refuge. The nearest town and the nearest Federal highway are 28 miles away. Primary access is by narrow, rough County road. This isolation gives the Refuge a unique quality of solitude considered very desirable by most of the 7,000 to 9,000 people who visit annually. The Proposed Wilderness Area adds to and protects that quality.

Goal 11:   Provide visitors an opportunity to enjoy, learn about and utilize fish and wildlife in a setting that emphasizes an undisturbed natural environment and minimum human interaction.

Objective: Designate an environmental education site for use by teachers and students which represents a cross-section of Refuge habitats.

Strategy:
- Provide facilities needed for the education process, minimize the area affected, and protect Refuge resources.

Objective: Establish one, perhaps two, interpretive walking trails with a total length of about two miles; add pullouts to the existing auto tour route; and upgrade the exhibits at the Refuge headquarters.

There are no interpretive walking trails on the Refuge. The existing auto tour route is on the County road, the only road passable to two-wheel drive vehicles year-round; it is not ideal for a quality interpretive experience. Adding pullouts to the existing roads could provide safer, more interesting experience, and could also provide access to the walking trails. Any new route would require expensive upgrades to be passable to all vehicles. The exhibits in and around Refuge headquarters are old and should be upgraded.

Strategy:
- Prepare a public use plan to: identify sites; determine feasibility, capacity and compatibility; and estimate costs (this strategy applies all public uses).

Fishing

Objectives: Continue to provide the year-round, warm water fishing in a largely natural setting presently offered on Island Lake and winter fishing at Smith and Crane Lakes (see Fish and Wildlife Objectives).

Impose use limits if more than 100 anglers per day commonly use any one lake.

Strategies:
- Continue the informal agreement with the Nebraska Game and Parks Commission for their involvement as the primary fishery manager.
- Conduct public use surveys to assure the number of anglers does not detract from the natural setting and feeling of relative isolation; use tools to control angler numbers, such as reduction of bag limits, or catch-and-release fishing, if necessary; a permit system would only be used as a last resort.

Hunting

Objective: Expand hunting to include limited waterfowl hunting.

The Refuge is now open to hunting for sharp-tailed grouse, pheasants, and deer. Expanding hunting to include waterfowl would provide additional public enjoyment without interfering with the sense of isolation so important to many users. It would also make hunting on Crescent Lake Refuge more consistent with the two other national wildlife refuges in the State. The expansion would require a Compatibility Determination and a revision of the present Hunting Plan; additional public involvement would be part of that process.

The relatively small amount of public use (about 8,000 visitors per year) is concentrated in time and space. For instance, seasonal hunting and fishing account for about 70 percent of this use. Most hunting occurs on a few opening weekends in the fall and the largest concentration occurs on opening weekend of deer season (about 60 hunters in recent years). Fishing is limited to three lakes. Aside from these concentrations, the Refuge is underutilized.

Strategies:
- Open waterfowl hunting on a limited area and prevent conflict with fall and winter fishing.

Objective: Limit overall hunting to fewer than 150 hunters on any one day; maintain the present aesthetic qualities of the hunting experience.

While current peak use is about half of this estimated maximum figure, growth should not be allowed to continue until a problem exists. Aesthetics is important to most hunters now using the Refuge and an integral part of Refuge objectives.

Strategy:
- Monitor all public use, obtain continuous feedback from hunters, and amend the Hunting Plan to include specific procedures.

Cultural Resources

Historic, archaeological, and paleontological resources on Crescent Lake Refuge are the responsibility of the Service. A review of existing information about archaeological and other cultural resources was conducted in 1999 (Burgett and Nickel 1999). Little systematic work has been conducted within the Nebraska Sandhills, and none is known on the Refuge. Individual sites affected by management activities are surveyed prior to disturbance.

Goal 12: Preserve the cultural resources of Crescent Lake Refuge.

Objective: Identify and protect cultural resources for scientific, educational, and interpretive purposes.

> Strategies:
> - Conduct a Refuge-wide survey to determine the presence of cultural resources on the Refuge when funded under RONS program.
> - After completion of the survey, prepare a cultural resources management plan which includes protection, interpretation, and educational use.
> - Continue to conduct site-specific surveys for lands and facilities that will be disturbed by refuge management activities; take advantage of prescribed burns and wildfires to detect the presence of cultural resources.

Lands and Facilities

The projects listed in the Service-wide Maintenance Management System (MMS) and the Refuge Operations Needs System (RONS) include those needed for protection of lands and facilities (see Appendix D). A few are highlighted here because they bear directly on the other objectives in this Plan and/or involve safety of employees.

Goal 13: Protect all government lands and facilities; eliminate unnecessary facilities.

Objective: Protect headquarters buildings, equipment, and residences from wildfires.

The headquarters area is vulnerable to wildfire, especially from the west. The area is remote and local fire departments could not be on the site in less than 30 minutes. Rough terrain and cedar windbreaks west of headquarters would make control very difficult even with wildland fire pumper units.

> Strategies:
> - Cover all buildings with fire resistant exteriors.
> - Store all firewood and flammable materials well away from buildings.
> - Keep vegetation within 50 feet of buildings mowed short.
>   (Note: Firebreaks are not an option in naturally vegetated areas of the Sandhills because repeated mowing or plowing results in blowing and large-scale wind erosion).

Objective: Remove unnecessary grazing management facilities.

Grazing practices have changed over the years and some windmills and fences can be removed. Such facilities require maintenance and detract from the aesthetic qualities of the Refuge, particularly in the Proposed Wilderness Area. Windmills are needed to provide water for firefighting and should be better distributed for that purpose. Service roads should be minimized.

Community Involvement / Support Systems

Goal 14:   Interact with communities and organizations to create mutually beneficial partnerships.

Objective: Maintain existing partnerships and agreements, and add others that will strengthen management of the Refuge and contribute to surrounding communities.

Strategies:

- Encourage and support scientific research, with emphasis on information needs of the Refuge.
- Participate with other Fish and Wildlife Service divisions and the State in the "ecosystem approach to resource management" and define the Refuge role in that effort.
- Participate in planning efforts at the State and local levels.
- Continue interagency cooperation in such activities as wildfire and noxious weed control.

Lands of Interest

Goal 15:   Protect important wildlife and endangered plant habitat surrounding the Refuge.

The Refuge, within the Nebraska sandhills, is not an island capable of supporting all wildlife during all seasons of the year. Much of the wildlife that use the Refuge also use, and to varying degrees are dependent on, wetlands and upland habitats on surrounding private lands. For instance, ducks that use Refuge wetlands as breeding pair habitat may nest across the fence on private lands, or vice versa. And sharp-tailed grouse that breed and nest on the Refuge may winter on private lands, sometimes several miles away. Thus, additional protection for habitats surrounding the Refuge would help assure that present numbers and distribution of wildlife can be sustained into the future.

To achieve the stated goals of endangered species, fish and wildlife, upland habitat, wetland habitat, and public use, land acquisition is not needed at this time. However, some areas surrounding the Refuge have the potential to secure habitat for the protection of trust species, such as the endangered blowout penstemon, which may contain small populations and would be considered for additional transplanting efforts.

Additional protection can be achieved in several ways: perpetual conservation easements; short-term agreements for specific actions or projects; and fee-title acquisition. In all cases, the additional protection would be acquired only from willing sellers. Further, no formal steps can be taken until the FWS completes a Preliminary Project Proposal, for the USFWS Director's approval, which specifically delineates the resources for which additional protection should be considered. National Environmental Policy Act requirements must also be met, which include additional public involvement.

Conservation easements offer permanent protection but leave the land in private ownership and, depending on the conditions of the easement, do not inhibit present economic uses of that land. Some of the basic types of easements are:

(1) wetlands easements which assure wetlands will not be drained or filled;

(2) grassland easements which assure grasslands will not be converted to farmland or other uses, but allow grazing and haying to continue; and

(3) a general easement which protects all lands within a given area from conversion to other uses.

Short-term agreements are offered under a FWS program, Partners For Fish and Wildlife. These agreements are usually for some specific management action such as changing the method or season of grazing to protect nesting birds or protecting or restoring stream banks from erosion caused by cattle grazing.

It is a vision of Refuge staff to evaluate habitat protection measures at a future date that may add to the protection of trust resources and add to the biological diversity of the sandhills surrounding the Crescent Lake Refuge. The following areas would be considered to study in more detail as a protection strategy for wildlife and endangered plant habitat surrounding the Refuge:

✓ The area west of Black Steer Lake is an area where blowout penstemon either exists or could exist.

✓ The area that surrounds Black Steer Lake which is an important area for trumpeter swans and other waterfowl.

✓ The area that includes Crescent Lake, Blue Lake, and a section of Nebraska School Land. These lakes are valuable wetlands for migratory birds.

✓ The area west of Upper Harrison Lake either has or could have blowout penstemon and should be protected.

✓ The area that includes Swan Lake, Lower Harrison Lake, and subirrigated meadows. It is important habitat for wetland birds.

✓ The area that includes Border Lake and Bean Lake is important for migratory birds, especially shorebirds. Also, the area either has or could have blowout penstemon.

✓ The area that includes Rush Lake is valuable migratory bird habitat and supports a second population of yellow mud turtle. This is the only other large population of yellow mud turtle in the area.

V. Implementation and Monitoring

Funding and Personnel
Staffing Needed for Implementation
The following staffing chart shows current staff and additional staffing needed to implement this Plan. All personnel would be part of the Crescent Lake National Wildlife Refuge Complex and some positions would be shared with the North Platte Refuge. If positions are not filled, some aspects of this Plan would not be completed or may take longer to complete.

Position	Current	Proposed
Project Leader *	X	X
Refuge Manager	X	X
Wildlife Biologist #		X
Refuge Operations Specialist		X
Outdoor Recreation Planner *		X
Administrative Support Assistant *	X	X
Engineering Equipment Operator #	X	X
Maintenance Worker	X	X
Fire Program Technician	X	X
Fire Management Officer / LE #		X
Maintenance Worker		X
Biological Aid		X
Range Technicians (fire / seasonal)	X(4)	X(5)

* Shared in the Complex and stationed at Scottsbluff
\# Shared in the Complex and stationed at Crescent Lake Refuge

Funding Needed for Implementation
The Service maintains two national databases for tracking funding needs: (1) The Maintenance Management System (MMS) which records needs for maintaining or replacing existing facilities and equipment; and (2) the Refuge Operating Needs System (RONS) which documents new or additional projects, facilities, equipment, and personnel needed to implement CCPs.

The Crescent Lake maintenance backlog was $4,437,000 in 2000 (see Appendix D for a project summary). New projects, or additions to existing projects, needed to fully implement this Plan total $2,244,000. Projects on both lists are in priority order as viewed by the Project Leader. Those priorities are sometimes changed as funding requests move up through the Service to the Department of the Interior and Congress. More specific information about each project can be found in the database on file at the Refuge headquarters.

Refuge Management Policies and Guidelines
In addition to the laws, policies, and regulations under which all national wildlife refuges operate, Crescent Lake Refuge is guided by a number of agreements with State and local agencies (see Section I and Appendix C). The public involvement/scoping process did not reveal a need to change these agreements.

Partnership Opportunities

The Service and Crescent Lake Refuge will continue to seek opportunities to work with Federal, State and local agencies, conservation groups, and private corporations and organizations to advance the purpose of the Refuge and the community. For instance, if bison are reintroduced, there may be opportunities for cooperative herd management. Also, there are many gaps in the biological database, and the Refuge will seek university-level research and management studies to help fill those gaps. Volunteer partnerships to assist with surveys, environmental education, and other activities are always needed although the remoteness of the Refuge limits such opportunities. Partnerships are, and will continue to be, an important part of future Refuge operations.

The Service is currently working with Garden County to improve the County road accessing the Refuge from the north and south. Improving this road will not only provide better access to the Refuge for the visiting public but will also benefit local residents who use the road for commercial agricultural business and fire protection.

Monitoring and Evaluation

This Plan emphasizes the importance of monitoring and evaluating the effects of applied management and public use on plants and animals. Additional scientific, long-term monitoring is needed in order to measure progress toward stated objectives, detect successes and failures, make adjustments in management techniques, and modify plans and budget requests. Some monitoring needs and techniques are documented in the step-down plans; others have been identified but not designed.

At this writing, a lot goes undone. The above staffing plan will contribute significantly to monitoring and evaluation and to conducting refuge management studies, but the Refuge staff will also be dependent on university level research and volunteers to get the whole job done right.

Plan Amendment and Revision

This is a dynamic Plan and will be adjusted to include new and better information. It will be monitored continuously, reviewed during inspections and programmatic evaluations, dove-tailed with budget requests and annual work plans, and formally reviewed every five years. Public involvement will be part of any substantive change. The Plan will be formally revised at least every 15 years.

Environmental Action Statement

U.S. Fish & Wildlife Service
Region 6
Denver, Colorado

Within the spirit and intent of the Council on Environmental Quality's regulations for implementing the National Environmental Policy Act (NEPA) and other statutes, orders, and policies that protect fish and wildlife resources, I have established the following administrative record and have determined that the action of implementing the Crescent Lake National Wildlife Refuge Comprehensive Conservation Plan (CCP) is found not to have significant environmental effects as determined by the attached Finding of No Significant Impact and the Environmental Assessment as found in the Draft CCP.

_8/19/02_
Ralph O. Morgenweck, Regional Director   Date
Region 6, U.S. Fish & Wildlife Service

_8/15/02_
Richard A. Coleman, Ph.D.   Date
Regional Chief, National Wildlife Refuge System
Refuges and Wildlife

_8-15-02_
Ron Cole, Refuge Program Supervisor   Date
National Wildlife Refuge System
Refuges and Wildlife

August 12, 2002
Steven A. Knode, Project Leader   Date
Crescent Lake / North Platte NWR Complex

Finding of No Significant Impact

Crescent Lake National Wildlife Refuge
Comprehensive Conservation Plan

Four management alternatives for the Crescent Lake National Wildlife Refuge were assessed as to their effectiveness in achieving the Refuge's purposes and their impact on the human environment. Alternative 1 - No Action Alternative which would continue the current management for the Refuge and not include extensive restoration of wetland and grassland habitats; Alternative 2 - historical management of refuge habitats and wildlife to replicate pre-settlement conditions; Alternative 3 - the intensive management of refuge habitats and refuge program to increase outputs in certain areas; and the preferred Alternative 4 - modified historical management of habitats for native birds and wild animals and to pursue a more natural historic management regime. The alternatives were assessed in the CCP management plan and Environmental Assessment. Based on this assessment and comments received, I have selected preferred Alternative 4 for implementation.

The preferred alternative was selected because it best meets the purposes of the Refuge to reserve and set apart as a refuge and breeding ground for birds and wild animals. The preferred alternative will also provide for public access for wildlife-dependent recreation, and provides environmental education opportunities related to fish and wildlife resources.

I find that the preferred Alternative is not a major Federal action that would significantly affect the quality of the human environment within the meaning of Section 102(2)(C) of the National Environmental Policy Act of 1969. Accordingly, the preparation of an environmental impact statement on the proposed action is not required.

Based on public comment and Service review of the Draft CCP, the following changes are noted to the Environmental Assessment published with the Draft CCP.

- Within the social economic conditions section of the EA, a comment was received stating that the Service did not identify there would be grazing income from privately owned bison. The Service agreed with this comment. The original Draft CCP anticipated a government owned bison herd; however, the Service's policy made this option very difficult so the idea of a privately owned bison herd was used as the most likely scenario.

- A comment was received requesting that the air quality class be addressed. The Refuge staff found that Nebraska has Class 2 air quality. While researching the air quality, we incorrectly stated there would be no effect on the air quality when in fact we should have said that any impacts to air quality would be short-term and will not exceed National Ambient Air Quality Standards.

- During the development and review of the Draft CCP, a neighboring landowner requested a land exchange of 200 acres with the Refuge. The Service approved the exchange for the following reasons. The Refuge exchanged land had bisected neighboring landowner property. Both of the exchanged parcels were similar vegetation types and of equal value. The exchange reduced maintenance cost for both the Refuge and neighboring landowner and improved ability to move grazing animals. The exchange is located within Township 21 North, Range 43 West, in Sections 24 and 25. The exchange and new Refuge boundary are reflected on the maps in the CCP.

- A comment was received indicating that while the Refuge has adequate personnel to cover most wildfires in the summer, they do not have those people employed during the fall and winter.

The following is a summary of anticipated environmental effects from implementation of the preferred alternative:

- The preferred alternative will not adversely impact endangered of threatened species or their habitat.

- The preferred alternative will not adversely impact archaeological or historical resources.

- The preferred alternative will not adversely impact wetlands nor does the plan call for structures that could be damaged by or that would significantly influence the movement of floodwater.

- The preferred alternative will not will have a disproportionately high or adverse human health or environmental effect on minority or low-income populations.

- The State of Nebraska has been notified and given the opportunity to review the Comprehensive Conservation Plan and associated Environmental Assessment.

Ralph O. Morgenweck   _8/19/02_

Regional Director, Region 6   Date
U.S. Fish & Wildlife Service
Denver, Colorado

Appendix A. Glossary (including acronyms and abbreviations)

Adaptive Management: Refers to the process in which policy decisions are implemented within a framework of scientifically driven experiments to test predictions and assumptions inherent in management plans. Analysis of results help managers to determine whether current management should continue as is or it should be modified to achieve desired conditions.

Alternative: 1) A reasonable way to fix the identified problem or satisfy the stated need (40 CFR 1500.2); 2) Alternatives are different means of accomplishing refuge purposes and goals and contributing to the System mission (Draft Service Manual 602 FW 1.5).

ATV: All Terrain Vehicle (either 3 or 4-wheeled vehicles)

AUM or Animal Unit Month: A measure of the quantity of livestock forage. Equivalent to the forage sufficient to sustain a 1,000 pound animal (or 1 cow/calf pair) for 1 month during a normal season.

Biological Control: The use of organisms or viruses to control weeds or other pests.

Biological Diversity: The variety of life and its processes, including the variety of living organisms, the genetic differences among them, and the communities and ecosystems in which they occur.

Categorical Exclusion (CE, CX, CATEX, CATX): A category of actions that do not individually or cumulatively have a significant effect on the human environment and have been found to have no such effect in procedures adopted by a Federal agency pursuant to the National Environmental Policy Act (40 CFR 1508.4).

CCP or Plan: Comprehensive Conservation Plan

CFR: Code of Federal Regulations

Compatible Use: A wildlife-dependent recreational use or any other use of a refuge that, in the sound professional judgment of the Director, will not materially interfere with or detract from the fulfillment of the mission of the System or the purposes of the refuge.

Comprehensive Conservation Plan, Plan, or CCP: A document that describes the desired future conditions of the refuge and provides long-range guidance and management direction for the refuge manager to accomplish the purposes of the refuge, contribute to the mission of the System, and to meet other relevant mandates.

Cover Type: The present vegetation of an area.

Cultural Resources: The remains of sites, structures, or objects used by people in the past.

Cultural Resource Inventory: A professionally conducted study designed to locate and evaluate evidence of cultural resources present within a defined geographic area. Inventories may involve various levels, including background literature search, comprehensive field examination to identify all exposed physical manifestations of cultural resources, or sample inventory to project site distribution and density over a larger area. Evaluation of identified cultural resources to determine eligibility for the National Register follows the criteria found in .36 CFR 60.4 (Service Manual 614 FW 1.7).

Cultural Resource Overview: A comprehensive document prepared for a field office that discusses, among other things, its prehistory and cultural history, the nature and extent of known cultural resources, previous research, management objectives, resource management conflicts or issues, and a general statement on how program objectives should be met and conflicts resolved. An overview should reference or incorporate information from a field offices background or literature search described in Section VIII of the Cultural Resource Management Handbook (Service Manual 614 FW 1.7).

Designated Wilderness Area: An area designated by the United States Congress to be managed as part of the National Wilderness Preservation System (Draft Service Manual 610 FW 1.5).

Disturbance: Significant alteration of habitat structure or composition. May be natural (e.g., fire) or human-caused events (e.g., timber harvest).

EA or Environmental Assessment: A concise public document, prepared in compliance with the National Environmental Policy Act, that briefly discusses the purpose and need for an action, alternatives to such action, and provides sufficient evidence and analysis of impacts to determine whether to prepare and Environmental Impact Statement (EIS) or a Finding of No Significant Impact (FONSI).

Ecosystem: Dynamic and interrelated complex of plant and animal communities and their associated nonliving environment.

Ecosystem Approach: Protecting or restoring the natural function, structure, and species composition of an ecosystem, recognizing that all components are interrelated.

Endangered Species (Federal): A plant or animal species listed under the Endangered Species Act that is in danger or becoming extinct throughout all or a significant portion of its range.

Endangered Species (State): A plant or animal species in danger of becoming extinct or extirpated in an individual State within the near future if factors contributing to its decline continue. Populations of these species are at critically low levels or their habitats have been degraded or depleted to a significant degree.

Endemic Species: Plants or animals that occur naturally in a certain region and whose distribution is relatively limited to a particular locality.

Exotic and Invading Species (Noxious Weeds): Plant species designated by Federal or State law as generally possessing one or more of the following characteristics: aggressive or difficult to manage; parasitic; a carrier or host of serious insects or disease; or nonnative, new, or not common to the United States, according to the Federal Noxious Weed Act (PL 93-639), a noxious weed is one that causes disease or has adverse effects on man or his environment and therefore is detrimental to the agriculture and commerce of the United States and to the public health.

Fauna: All the vertebrate and invertebrate animal species of a determined area.

Federal Trust Resources: A trust is something managed by one entity for another who holds the ownership. The Service holds in trust many natural resources for the people of the United States of America as a result of Federal Acts and treaties. Examples are species listed under the Endangered Species Act, migratory birds protected by the Migratory Bird Treaty Act and other international treaties, and native plant or wildlife species found on the System.

Federal Trust Species: All species where the Federal government has primary jurisdiction including federally endangered or threatened species, migratory birds, anadromous fish, and certain marine mammals.

Fire Regime: A description of the frequency, severity, and extent of fire that typically occurs in an area or vegetative type.

Flora: All the plant species of a determined area.

FONSI or Finding of No Significant Impact: A document prepared in compliance with the National Environmental Policy Act, supported by an environmental assessment, that briefly presents why a Federal Action will have no significant effects on the human environment and for which an Environmental Impact Statement, therefore, will not be prepared (40 CFR 1508.13).

Forb: A broad-leaved, herbaceous plant; for example, a columbine.

Fragmentation: The process of reducing the size and connectivity of habitat patches.

Geographic Information System (GIS): A computer system capable of storing and manipulating spatial data.

Goal: Descriptive, open-ended, and often broad statement of desired future conditions that conveys a purpose but does not define measurable units (Draft Service Manual 620 FW 1.5).

Habitat: Suite of existing environmental conditions required by an organism for survival and reproduction. The place where an organism typically lives.

Habitat Restoration: Management emphasis designed to move ecosystems to desired conditions and processes, and/or to healthy forest lands, rangelands, and aquatic systems.

Integrated Pest Management: Methods of managing undesirable species, such as weeds, including: education; prevention, physical or mechanical methods of control; biological control; responsible chemical use; and cultural methods.

Issue: Any unsettled matter that requires a management decision; e.g., a Service initiative, opportunity, resource management problem, threat to the resources of the unit, conflict in uses, public concern, or the presence of an undesirable resource condition (Draft Service Manual 602 FW 1.5).

Migration: The seasonal movement from one area to another and back.

Minimum Tool: The minimum action or instrument necessary to successfully, safely and economically accomplish wilderness management objectives.

Mission Statement: A succinct statement of a unit's purpose and reason for being.

Mitigation: Measures designed to counteract environmental impacts or to make impacts less severe.

Monitoring: The process of collecting information to track changes of selected parameters over time.

National Wildlife Refuge (Refuge): A designated area of land or water or an interest in land or water within the System, including national wildlife refuges, wildlife ranges, wildlife management areas, waterfowl production areas, and other areas (except coordination areas) under Service jurisdiction for the protection and conservation of fish and wildlife. A complete listing of all units of the Refuge System may be found in the current "Annual Report of Lands Under Control of the U.S. Fish & Wildlife Service."

National Wildlife Refuge System, Refuge System, or System: Various categories of areas that are administered by the Secretary for the conservation of fish and wildlife, including species that are threatened with extinction; all lands, waters, and interests therein administered by the secretary as wildlife refuges; areas for the protection and conservation of fish and wildlife that are threatened with extinction; wildlife ranges; game ranges; wildlife management or waterfowl production areas.

Native Species: Species that normally live and thrive in a particular ecosystem.

Neotropical Migratory Bird or Neotropicals: A bird species that breeds north of the U.S. - Mexican border and winters primarily south of this border.

NEPA: National Environmental Policy Act of 1969

NGPC: Nebraska Game and Parks Commission

No Action Alternative: An alternative under which existing management would be continued.

Non-Priority Public Uses: Any use other than a compatible wildlife-dependent recreational use.

Notice of Availability or NOA: An NOA is a notice that documentation is available to the public on a Federal action, in this case, the Comprehensive Conservation Plan. Published in the Federal Register.

Notice of Intent or NOI: In the case of a Federal action, such as analyzed in this documentation, an NOI is a notice that an environmental impact statement will be prepared and considered (40 CFR 1508.22). Published in the Federal Register.

Noxious Weed: A plant species designated by Federal or State law as generally possessing one or more of the following characteristics: aggressive or difficult to manage; parasitic; a carrier or host of serious insect or disease; or nonnative, new, or not common to the United States, according to the Federal Noxious Weed Act (PL 93-639), a noxious weed is one that causes disease or had adverse effects on man or his environment and, therefore, is detrimental to the agriculture and commerce of the Untied States and to the public health.

NRCS: National Resource Conservation Service

NWR: National Wildlife Refuge

Objective: A concise statement of what will be achieved, how much will be achieved, when and where it will be achieved, and who is responsible for the work. Objectives are derived from goals and provide the basis for determining management strategies, monitoring refuge accomplishments, and evaluating the success of the strategies. Objectives should be attainable and time-specific and should be stated quantitatively to the extent possible. If objectives cannot be stated quantitatively, they may be stated qualitatively (Draft Service Manual 602 FW 1.5).

Opportunities: Potential solutions to issues.

Planning Area: A planning area may include lands outside existing planning unit boundaries that are being studied for inclusion in the System and/or partnership planning efforts. It may also include watersheds or ecosystems that affect the planning area.

Planning Team: A team or group of persons working together to prepare a document, such as this Comprehensive Conservation Plan. Planning teams are interdisciplinary in membership and function. Teams generally consist of a planning team leader; refuge manager and staff; biologists; staff specialists or other representatives of Service programs, ecosystems or regional offices; and other Federal and State governmental agencies as appropriate.

Planning Unit: A single refuge, an ecologically/administratively related complex of refuges, or distinct unit of a refuge.

Plant Community: An assemblage of plant species unique in its composition; occurs in particular locations under particular influences; a reflection or integration of the environmental influences on the site - such as soils, temperature, elevation, solar radiation, slope, aspect, and rainfall; denotes a general kind of climax plant community, i.e., ponderosa pine or bunch grass.

PILT: Payment-in-Lieu-of-Taxes

Prairie Grouse: both sharp-tailed grouse and prairie chickens.

Preferred Alternative: This is the alternative determined (by the decision-maker) to best achieve the Refuge purpose, vision, and goals; contributes to the Refuge System mission, addresses the significant issues; and is consistent with principles of sound fish and wildlife management. The Service's selected alternative at the draft CCP stage.

Prescribed Fire: The skillful application of fire to natural fuels under conditions of weather, fuel moisture, soil moisture, etc., that allows confinement of the fire to a predetermined area and produces the intensity of heat and rate of spread to accomplish planned benefits to one or more objectives of habitat management, wildlife management, or hazard reduction.

Priority Public Uses: Compatible wildlife-dependent recreational uses (hunting, fishing, wildlife observation and photography, and environmental education and interpretation) are the priority general public uses of the System and shall receive priority consideration in refuge planning and management.

Proposed Action: The Service's proposed action for Comprehensive Conservation Plans is to prepare and implement the CCP.

Public: Individuals, organizations, and groups; officials of Federal, State, and local government agencies; Indian tribes; and foreign nations. It may include anyone outside the core planning team. It includes those who may or may not have indicated an interest in Service issues and those who do or do not realize that Service decisions may affect them.

Public Involvement: The process by which interested and affected individuals, organizations, agencies, and governmental entities are offered an opportunity to become informed about, to express their opinions and participate in the planning and decision-making process of Service actions and policies. In this process, these views are studied thoroughly and thoughtful consideration of public views is given in shaping decisions for refuge management.

Purposes of the Refuge: The purposes specified in or derived from the law, proclamation, executive order, agreement, public land order, donation document, or administrative memorandum establishing, authorizing, or expanding a refuge, refuge unit, or refuge sub-unit.

ROD or Record of Decision: A concise public record of decision prepared by the Federal agency, pursuant to the National Environmental Policy Act, that contains a statement of the decision, identification of all alternatives considered, identification of the environmentally preferable alternative, a statement as to whether all practical means to avoid or minimize environmental harm from the alternative selected have been adopted (and if not, why they were not adopted), and a summary of monitoring and enforcement where applicable for any mitigation (40 CFR 1505.2).

Refuge: short for Crescent Lake National Wildlife Refuge

Refuge Operating Needs System or RONS: National database containing the unfunded operational needs of each refuge. Projects included are those required to implement approved plans, and meet goals, objectives, and legal mandates.

Refuge Purposes: The purposes specified in or derived from the law, proclamation, executive order, agreement, public land order, donation document, or administrative memorandum establishing, authorizing, or expanding a refuge, a refuge unit, or refuge sub-unit (Draft Service Manual 602 FW 1.5)

Refuge Revenue Share Program or RASP: Provides payments to counties in lieu of taxes using revenues derived from the sale of products from refuges (see Appendix C. Refuge Revenue Sharing Act of 1935, as amended (16 U.S.C. 715s) for more details).

Refuge Use: Any activity on a refuge, except administrative or law enforcement activity carried out by or under the direction of an authorized Service employee.

Reserve Acres: Lands that were Public Domain lands when first withdrawn to create the Refuge.

Riparian: Refers to an area or habitat that is transitional from terrestrial to aquatic ecosystems; including streams, lakes, wet areas, and adjacent plant communities and their associated soils which have free water at or near the surface; and area whose components are directly or indirectly attributed to the influence of water; of or relating to a river; specifically applied to ecology, "riparian" describes the land immediately adjoining and directly influenced by streams. For example, riparian vegetation includes any and all plant-life growing on the land adjoining a stream and directly influenced by the stream.

Secretary: short for Secretary of Interior

Service or USFWS: Short for U.S. Fish & Wildlife Service

Special Status Species: Plants or animals which have been identified through either Federal law, State law, or agency policy, as requiring special protection of monitoring. Examples include federally listed endangered, threatened, proposed, or candidate species; state listed endangered, threatened, candidate, or monitor species; U.S. Fish & Wildlife Service species of management concern and species identified by the Partners in Flight program as being of extreme or moderately high conservation concern.

Species of Management Interest: Those plant and animal species, while not failing under the definition of special status species, that are of management interest by virtue of being Federal trust species such as migratory birds, important game species including white-tailed deer, furbearers such as American marten, important prey species including red-backed vole, or significant keystone species such as beaver.

Strategy: A specific action, tool, or technique or combination of actions, tools, and techniques used to meet refuge objectives.

Step-Down Management Plan: A plan that provides the details necessary to implement strategies identified in the CCP. (Draft Service Manual 602 FW 1.5).

Sound Professional Judgement: A finding, determination, or decision that is consistent with principles of sound fish and wildlife management and administration, available science and resources, and adherence to the requirements of the Refuge Administration Act and other applicable laws.

Strategy: A specific action, tool, or technique or combination of actions, tools, and techniques used to meet unit objectives (Draft Service Manual 602 FW 1.5).

System or Refuge System: National Wildlife Refuge System

Threatened Species (Federal): Species listed under the Endangered Species Act that are likely to become endangered within the foreseeable future throughout all or a significant portion of their range.

Threatened Species (State): A plant or animal species likely to become endangered in an individual State within the near future if factors contributing to population decline or habitat degradation or loss continue.

Trust Species: Species for which the U.S. Fish & Wildlife Service has primary responsibility, including, most federally-listed threatened and endangered species, anadromous fishes once they enter inland U.S. waterways, migratory birds, and certain marine mammals.

USFWS or Service: Short for U.S. Fish & Wildlife Service

Vegetation Type or Habitat Type: A land classification system based upon the concept of distinct plant associations.

Vision Statement: A concise statement of the desired future condition of the planning unit, based primarily upon the System mission, specific refuge purposes, and other relevant mandates (Draft Service Manual 602 FW 1.5).

VORS: Visual Observation Readings. A measurement of the density of a plant community; the height of vegetation that blocks the view of predators to a nest.

Wetland: includes lakes, marshes, temporary wetlands, fens, rivers, and creeks but not subirrigated meadows.

Wilderness Area (or Designated Wilderness Area): An area designated by the U.S. Congress to be managed as part of the National Wilderness Preservation System (Draft Service Manual 602 FW 1.5).

Wildfire: A free-burning fire requiring a suppression response; all fire other than prescribed fire that occurs on wildlands (Draft Service Manual 602 FW 1.5).

Wildland: lands characterized by natural vegetation and landscapes where man-made structures and alterations are not evident.

Wildland Fire: Every wildland fire is either a wildfire or a prescribed fire (Draft Service Manual 602 FW 1.5).

Wildlife: Wild animals and vegetation, especially animals living in a natural, undomesticated state.

Wildlife Corridor: A landscape feature that facilitates the biologically effective transport of animals between larger patches of habitat dedicated to conservation functions. Such corridors may facilitate several kinds of traffic, including frequent foraging movement, seasonal migration, or the once in a lifetime dispersal of juvenile animals. These are transition habitats and need not contain all the habitat elements required for long-term survival or reproduction of its migrants.

Wildlife-Dependent Recreation/Wildlife-Dependent Recreational Use: A use of a refuge involving hunting, fishing, wildlife observation and photography, or environmental education and interpretation. The National Wildlife Refuge System Improvement Act of 1997 specifies that these are the six priority general public uses of the System.

Appendix B. Literature Cited / References

Bandy, Mollie.1980. A Study of Upland Sandpiper Behavior and Habitat Selection in the Sandhills of Nebraska. Univ. Of Nebr., Omaha. Masters thesis. 62 pp.

Barnes, P.W. 1984 Vegetation patterns in relation to topography and edaphic variation in Nebraska Sandhills Prairie. Prairie Nat. 16(4): 145-158.

Bicak, T.K. 1977. Some Eco-ethological Aspects of a Breeding Population of Long-billed Curlews in Nebraska, Proc. Nebr. Acad. Sci. Affil. Soc. 87:7

Bleed, A. and C. Flowerday, Ed. 1989. An Atlas of the Sandhills, Sec. Edition. Cons. And Survey Div., Insti. Of Agr. And Natural Resources, Univ. Of Nebr.-Lincoln. 265 pp.

Bue, I.G. 1952. The Relationship of Grazing Practices to Waterfowl Breeding Populations and Production on Stock Ponds in Western South Dakota. Trns. N. Am. Wildl. Conf. 17:396-414.

Burgett, G.R. and R.K. Nickel. 1999. Archeological Overview and Assessment for Lacreek, Fort Niobrara and Valentine National Wildlife Refuges. Midwest Archeological Center, National Park Service. 41pp.

Christisen, D.M. 1969. National Status and Management of the Greater Prairie Chicken. Trans. N. Amer. Wildl. and Nat. Resour. Conf. 34:207-217.

Clark, J.P. 1977. Effects of Experimental Management Schemes on Production and Nesting Ecology of Ducks at Malheur National Wildlife Refuge. Oregon State University Masters Thesis. 79 pp.

Duebbert, H.F. 1966 Island Nesting of the Gadwall in North Dakota. Wilson Bull. 78:12-25.

Duebbert, H.F. 1969 High nest density and hatching success of ducks on South Dakota CAP land. Trans. Of Am. Wildl. Resour. Conf. 34:218-229

Duebbert, H.F. 1974 Creating a Sea of Grass. Ducks Unlimited Magazine Mar-Apr 1974.

Duebbert, H.F. and J.T. Lokemoen. 1976 Duck nesting in fields of undisturbed grass-legume cover. J. Wildl. Manage. 40(1) :39-49.

Farrar, J. 1990. Wildflowers of Nebraska and the Great Plains. NEBRASKALand Magazine, Nebraska G.&P. Commission. 216 pp.

Fredrickson, L. 2001. Crescent Lake National Wildlife Refuge trip Report, September 19-20.

Fritz, M., J.S. Stubbendieck, and W. Jobman. 1992. Recovery Plan - Blowout Penstemon. 40 pp.

Gjersing, F.M. 1975. Wildlife Production in Relation to Rest-Rotation Grazing. J. Range Manage. 28(1): 37-42.

Hopton, J. 1996. Grasshopper Sparrow Habitat Selection in Garden County, Nebraska. Unpublished data. Crescent Lake NWR, Ellsworth, NE.

Hrabik, R.A. 1989. Fishes in An Atlas of the Sandhills. Resource Atlas No.5. Conservation and Survey Division. University of Nebraska - Lincoln. 265pp.

Imler, R.H. 1942. Waterfowl Nesting Studies and Experimental Bullsnake Control, Crescent Lake Refuge, Nebraska and Lacreek Refuge, South Dakota in 1940. Unpublished rept. U.S. Fish & Wildlife Service files. 37 pp.

Iverson, J. Annual Study Reports. unpublished data. Crescent Lake NWR, Ellsworth, NE.

Jones, J.K. 1964. Distribution and taxonomy of mammals of Nebraska. Univ. Of Kansas Publ., Museum of Natural History, 16:1-356.

Jones, R.E. 1963. Identification and Analysis of Lessor and Greater Prairie Chicken Habitat. J. Wildli. Manage. 27(4): 257-778.

Kantrud, H.A. 1982. R. Kologiski 1982. Effects of Soils and Grazing on Breeding Birds of Uncultivated Upland Grasslands of the Northern Great Plains. U.S. Fish and Wildl. Serv. Rep.: 15.ii+33 pp. WR 186.

Keeler, K.H., A.T. Harrison, and L.S. Vescio. 1980. The flora and sandhills prairie communities of Arapaho Prairie, Arthur County, Nebraska. Prairie Nat. 12:65-78.

Kirsch, L.M. and A.D. Kruse 1973. Proc. Tall Timbers Fire Ecology Conf. 12:289-303

Kirsch, L. M. 1973. Habitat Management Considerations for Prairie Chickens. Wildl. Soc. Bull. 2(3): 124-129.

Kirsch, L.M. 1978. Grazing and Haying Effects on Habitats of Upland Nesting Birds. Trans. of 43rd No. Am. Wildlife and Natural Resources Conf. 43:486-497.

LaGrange, T. 1997. Guide to Nebraska's wetlands and their conservation needs. Nebraska Game and Parks Commission, Lincoln, Nebraska. 34 pp.

Layton, M.H., C.R. Buzzard, and H.E. Hoy. 1956. A Soil Survey of Cherry County, Nebraska. U.S. Department of Agriculture, Soil Conservation Service. 91 pp.

Lehman, V.W. 1963. Status of Attwater's Prairie Chicken. J. Wildl. Manage. 27(4): 712-725

McMurtrey, M.S. and Robert Craig. 1969. Job no. K1. USFWS. 16 pp.

Natural Resource Conservation Service. 1995. Range Site and Condition Survey-Crescent Lake NWR. Unpublished data. Crescent Lake NWR, Ellsworth, NE.

Oosting, J.H. 1948. The study of plant communities. W.H. Freeman and Company. 440 pp.

Panhandle Area Development District. Undated (ca. 1998). Economic Development Report. Gering, NE. 10 pp.

Prairie Grouse Technical Conference. 1998. Unpublished proceedings. Crookston, MN.

Ryder, R.A. 1980. Effects of Grazing on Bird Habitats. U.S. For. Serv. Gen. Tech. Rep: Int-86:51-66.

Schwartz, C.W. 1945. The Ecology of the Prairie Chicken in Missouri. Univ. of Missouri Studies 20(1): 1-99.

Tolstead, W.L. 1942. Vegetation in the Northern Part of Cherry County, Nebraska. Ecol. Monog. 12:255-292.

U.S. Fish & Wildlife Service and Canadian Wildlife Service. 1986. North American Waterfowl Management Plan.

U.S. Fish & Wildlife Service.1986. Sandhills Wetlands-a Special Investigation. Unpublished document. 20 pp.

U.S. Fish & Wildlife Service.1982. Refuge Manual, 8RM 9.5 (B)

U.S. Fish & Wildlife Service. An ecosystem approach to fish and wildlife conservation. March 1994

Vichmeyer, G. 1941. The Present Status of the Greater Prairie Chicken and Sharp-tailed Grouse in the Sandhills Region of Nebraska. Nebr. Bird Rev. 9(1): 1-7

Wilhite, D.A. and K.G. Hubbard, 1989. Climate. Pages 17-28 in Breed, A. and Flowerday, C., Ed. Sec. Edition. An Atlas of the Sandhills. Cons. and Sur. Div., Insti. Agr. and Nat. Resource. Univ. Nebr.- Lincoln. 265 pp.

Yeatter, R.R. 1963. Population Responses of Prairie Chickens to Land Use Changes in Illinois. J. Wildl. Manage. 27(4) 739-757.

Additional References not Cited in Text

Belrose, F.S. 1980. Ducks, Geese, and Swans of North America. Stackpole books, Harrisburg, PA, 540 pp.

Boydeck, R.K. 1997 Habitat management for sharptail grouse on private lands in Manitoba, Canada. Wildlife Biology, Vol. 3/4.

Bragg, T.B. 1994 (in press). The physical environment of Great Plains Grasslands. From Keeler, K.A., A. Joren (editors), Oxford University Press, New York.

Hoffman, R.W. and G.M. Beauprez. 1997. Reintroduction of greater prairie chickens in north-central Colorado. Wildlife Biology Vol. 3/4

Kuzila, M. 1989. Soil association and series. in An Atlas of the Sandhills. Resource Publication 5. Conservation and Survey Division. University of Nebraska - Lincoln. 265pp.

Miller, S.M. 1990. Land development and use. in An atlas of the Sandhills. Resource Atlas No.5a. Conservation and Survey Division. University of Nebraska - Lincoln 265 pp.

Mitchell, L. and C. Wolfe. 1984. Prairie grouse in Nebraska. NEBRASKALand Magazine, Nebr. Game and Parks Comm. 15 pp.

Natural Resource Conservation Service. 1999. Soil Survey of Garden County Nebraska. 273 pp.

U.S. Fish & Wildlife Service. Valentine National Wildlife Refuge Draft Comprehensive Conservation Plan and Environmental Assessment. April 1999. 74 pp.

Weaver, J.E. 1961. The living network in prairie soils. The Botanical Gazette 123(1):16-28

Appendix C. Legal and Policy Guidance

Many procedural and substantive requirements of Federal and applicable State and local laws and regulations affect Refuge establishment, management, and development. This appendix identifies the key permits, approvals, and consultations needed to implement the strategies.

In undertaking the proposed action, the Service would comply with the following Federal laws, Executive orders, and legislative acts.

American Indian Religious Freedom Act of 1978: Directs agencies to consult with native traditional religious leaders to determine appropriate policy changes necessary to protect and preserve Native American religious cultural rights and practices.

Americans With Disabilities Act of 1992: Prohibits discrimination in public accommodations and services.

Antiquities Act of 1906: Authorizes the scientific investigation of antiquities on Federal land and provides penalties for unauthorized removal of objects taken or collected without a permit.

Archaeological and Historic Preservation Act of 1974: Directs the preservation of historic and archaeological data in Federal construction projects.

Archaeological Resources Protection Act of 1979, as amended: Protects materials of archaeological interest from unauthorized removal or destruction and requires Federal managers to develop plans and schedules to locate archaeological resources.

Architectural Barriers Act of 1968: Requires federally owned, leased, or funded buildings and facilities to be accessible to persons with disabilities.

Bald and Golden Eagle Protection Act of 1940, as amended: Calls for the protection of these raptorial species on and off Federal Lands.

Clean Air Act of 1977, as amended: The primary objective of this Act is to establish Federal standards for various pollutants from both stationary and mobile sources and to provide for the regulation of polluting emissions via state implementation plants. In addition, and of special interest for National Wildlife Refuges, some amendments are designed to prevent significant deterioration in certain areas where air quality exceeds national standards, and to provide for improved air quality in areas which do not meet Federal standards ('non-attainment' areas). Federal facilities are required to comply with air quality standards to the same extent as non-governmental entities (42 U.S.C. 7418). Part C of the 1977 amendments stipulates requirements to prevent significant deterioration of air quality and, in particular, to preserve air quality in national parks, National wilderness areas, national monuments, and national seashores (42 U.S.C. 7470).

Clean Water Act of 1977: Requires consultation with the Corps of Engineers (404 permits) for wetland modifications.

Emergency Wetlands Resources Act of 1986: The purpose of the Act is 'To promote the conservation of migratory waterfowl and to offset or prevent the serious loss of wetlands by the acquisition of wetlands and other essential habitat, and for other purposes.'

Endangered Species Act of 1973, as amended: Requires all Federal agencies to carry out programs for the conservation of endangered and threatened species. An Intra-Service Section 7 consultation was conducted prior to implementation of this CCP (as an appendix). No significant impact is expected from the implementation of this Plan.

Executive Order 11644, Use of Off-Road Vehicles on Public Lands.

Executive Order No. 11593, Protection and Enhancement of the Cultural Environment (1971). If the Service proposes any development activities that would affect the archaeological or historical sites, the Service will consult with Federal and State Historic Preservation Officers to comply with Section 106 of the National Historic Preservation Act of 1966, as amended.

Executive Order No. 11988, Floodplain Management. Each Federal agency shall provide leadership and take action to reduce the risk of flood loss and minimize the impact of floods on human safety, and preserve the natural and beneficial values served by the floodplains. No structures or other barriers that could either be damaged by or significantly influenced the movement of flood waters are planned for construction by the Service in the project area. This Plan supports the preservation and enhancement of the natural and beneficial values of floodplains.

Executive Order No. 11990, Protection of Wetlands. The proposal will help conserve the natural and beneficial values of the wetland habitat. The Service will undertake no activity that would be detrimental to the continuance of the vital wetlands.

Executive Order 13084, Consultation and Coordination with Indian Tribal Governments.

Executive Order No. 12372, Intergovernmental Review of Federal Programs. The State of Nebraska and counties encompassing the Refuge were sent copies of the Draft Comprehensive Conservation Plan and Environmental Assessment for distribution to State and County agencies and departments. Coordination and consultation is ongoing with local and State governments, Tribes, Congressional representatives, and other Federal agencies.

Executive Order No. 12898, Environmental Justice in Minority Populations and Low-income Populations. This environmental justice analysis concluded that the socio-economic, cultural, physical, and biological effects of the preferred alternative (the CCP) does not predict any outcomes that would cause disproportionately high and adverse human health impacts in any population, nor would they result in disproportionally high or adverse impact to low-income or minority populations, nor would create a greater burden on low-income households.

Executive Order 12996 Management and General Public Use of the National Wildlife Refuge System (1996): Defines the mission, purpose, and priority public uses of the National Wildlife Refuge System. It also presents four principles to guide management of the System. Through the development of this Comprehensive Conservation Plan, the Service has completed compatibility determinations for existing wildlife-dependent recreational activities that will be allowed to continue.

Executive Order 13007 Indian Sacred Sites (1996): Directs Federal land management agencies to accommodate access to and ceremonial use of Indian sacred sites by Indian religious practitioners, avoid adversely affecting the physical integrity of such sacred sites, and where appropriate, maintain the confidentiality of sacred sites.

Federal Noxious Weed Act of 1990: Requires the use of integrated management systems to control or contain undesirable plant species; and an interdisciplinary approach with the cooperation of other Federal and State agencies.

Fish and Wildlife Act of 1956: Established a comprehensive national fish and wildlife policy and broadened the authority for acquisition and development of refuges.

Fish and Wildlife Coordination Act of 1958: Allows the Fish and Wildlife Service to enter into agreements with private landowners for wildlife management purposes.

Land and Water Conservation Fund Act of 1965: Uses the receipts from the sale of surplus Federal land, outer continental shelf oil and gas sales, and other sources for land acquisition under several authorities.

Migratory Bird Conservation Act of 1929: Establishes procedures for acquisition by purchase, rental, or gift of areas approved by the Migratory Bird Conservation Commission.

Migratory Bird Hunting and Conservation Stamp Act (1934): Authorized the opening of part of a refuge to waterfowl hunting.

Migratory Bird Treaty Act of 1918: Designates the protection of migratory birds as a Federal responsibility. This Act enables the setting of seasons, and other regulations including the closing of areas, Federal or non-Federal, to the hunting of migratory birds.

National Environmental Policy Act of 1969 (40 CFR 1500): Requires all Federal agencies to examine the impacts upon the environment that their actions might have, to incorporate the best available environmental information, and the use of public participation in the planning and implementation of all actions. All Federal agencies must integrate NEPA with other planning requirements, and prepare appropriate NEPA documentation to facilitate sound environmental decision-making. NEPA requires the disclosure of the environmental impacts of any major Federal action that affects in a significant way the quality of the human environment. The process, from its inception, to prepare this Plan complied with all of NEPA requirements.

National Historic Preservation Act of 1966, as amended: Establishes as policy that the Federal Government is to provide leadership in the preservation of the nation's prehistoric and historic resources. The State of Nebraska's State Historic Preservation Officer will be consulted prior to removal of the present bunkhouse to be replaced with a new building. This house was constructed by the CCC in the 1930s to serve as the manager's residence and office.

National Wildlife Refuge System Administration Act of 1966 as amended by the National Wildlife Refuge System Improvement Act of 1997, 16 U.S.C. 668dd-668ee. (Refuge Administration Act): Defines the National Wildlife Refuge System and authorizes the Secretary to permit any use of a refuge provided such use is compatible with the major purposes for which the refuge was established. The Refuge Improvement Act clearly defines a unifying mission for the Refuge System; establishes the legitimacy and appropriateness of the six priority public uses (hunting, fishing, wildlife observation and photography, or environmental education and interpretation); establishes a formal process for determining compatibility; established the responsibilities of the Secretary of Interior for managing and protecting the System; and requires the preparation and implementation of a Comprehensive Conservation Plan for each refuge by the year 2012. This Act amended portions of the Refuge Recreation Act and National Wildlife Refuge System Administration Act of 1966. This Plan is in compliance with the National Wildlife Refuge System Act of 1966, as amended.

Native American Graves Protection and Repatriation Act of 1990: Requires Federal agencies and museums to inventory, determine ownership of, and repatriate cultural items under their control or possession. No known Native American cultural items are known to exist or are in possession of the Refuge.

Refuge Recreation Act of 1962, as amended: Allows the use of refuges for recreation when such uses are compatible with the refuge's primary purposes and when sufficient funds are available to manage the uses. This Plan is in compliance with the Refuge Recreation Act.

Refuge Revenue Sharing Act of 1935, as amended (16 U.S.C. 715s): provides for payments to counties in lieu of taxes, using revenues derived from the sale of products from refuges. Public Law 88-523 (1964) revised this Act and required that all revenues received from refuge products, such as animals, timber and minerals, or from leases or other privileges, be deposited in a special Treasury account and net receipts distributed to counties for public schools and roads. Payments to counties were established as: 1) on acquired land, the greatest amount calculated on the basis of 75 cents per acre, three-fourths of one percent of the appraised value, or 25 percent of the net receipts produced from the land; and 2) on land withdrawn from the public domain, 25 percent of net receipts and basic payments under Public Law 94-565 (31 U.S.C. 1601-1607, 90 Stat. 2662), payment in lieu of taxes on public lands. The current and proposed management of this Refuge under this Plan is in compliance with this Act.

Rehabilitation Act of 1973: Requires programmatic accessibility in addition to physical accessibility for all facilities and programs funded by the Federal government to ensure that anybody can participate in any program.

Secretarial Order 3127 (602 DM 2) Contaminants and Hazardous Waste Determination. No contaminants or hazardous waste are known to exist on the Refuge and none will be created.

Volunteer and Community Partnership Enhancement Act (1998): The purposes of this Act are to encourage the use of volunteers to assist in the management of refuges within the Refuge System; to facilitate partnerships between the Refuge System and non-Federal entities to promote public awareness of the resources of the Refuge System and public participation in the conservation of the resources and; to encourage donations and other contributions.

Wilderness Act of 1964 (Public Law 88-577 [16 U.S. C. 1131-1136]): defines wilderness as follows: "A wilderness, in contrast with those areas where man and his works dominate the landscape, is hereby recognized as an area where the earth and its community of life are untrammeled by man, where man himself is a visitor who does not remain. An area of wilderness is further defined to mean in this Act an area of undeveloped Federal land retaining its primeval character and influence, without permanent improvements or human habitation, which is protected and managed so as to preserve its natural conditions and which (1) generally appears to have been affected primarily by the forces of nature, with the imprint of man's work substantially unnoticeable; (2) has outstanding opportunities for solitude or a primitive and unconfined type of recreation; (3) has at least 5,000 acres of land or is of sufficient size as to make practicable its preservation and use in an unimpaired condition; and (4) may also contain ecological, geological, or other features of scientific, educational, scenic, or historical value."

Appendix D. Operation and Maintenance Needs

RONS

The Refuge Operation Needs System (RONS) is a comprehensive, Service-wide database containing the unfunded operational needs of each refuge. The following list of projects for the Crescent Lake NWR, in priority order, are those required to implement approved plans, and meet goals, objectives, and legal mandates. More specific information about each project can be found in the database on file at the Refuge headquarters.

*   Complex denotes project or MMS need is shared with North Platte NWR

** Only after Objective to reintroduce bison is accepted and conditions met as outlined in the Fish and Wildlife Section under the "reintroduce bison" objective

Refuge Operation Needs System (RONS) Projects			
Project	Links to CCP Goal	FTE Cost (2000 dollars)	Other Costs (2000 dollars)
Biologist - Complex *	1-10, 15	$58,000	$75,000
Assistant Refuge Manager	1-15	48,000	75,000
Maintenance Position	1-15	43,000	75,000
Public Use Specialist	11, 12, 14	58,000	80,000
Blowout Penstemon Habitat	1-4, 7, 8, 15	16,000	66,000
Noxious Weed Control	1-8, 10		50,000
Wilderness Area Restoration	1-4, 8, 11, 13, 14	17,000	155,000
Office/Visitor Center Expansion	11, 14		85,000
Seasonal Firefighters	1-10, 12-15	177,000	84,000
Grassland Study	1-10	20,000	34,000
Bison Reintroduction **	1-8, 10, 11, 14	39,000	241,000
Law Enforcement Center	1-15	52,000	75,000
Habitat Mgt - Wet Meadows	4, 5, 8, 10	16,000	51,000
Habitat Mgt - Wetlands	4, 9, 11	43,000	77,000
Carp Control	4, 9, 14, 15	16,000	500,000
Archaeological Inventory	12, 14		255,000
TOTALS		$603,000	$1,978,000

MMS

The Maintenance Management System (MMS) documents, Service-wide, facility and equipment deficiencies, justifies budget requests for maintenance needs, and provides a basis for management decision-making. The Crescent Lake NWR maintenance backlog is $3,339,000. The following MMS projects for the Refuge are listed in priority order. MMS projects not related to this document are not shown here. More specific information about each maintenance need can be found in the database on file at the Refuge headquarters.

Priority MMS Needs and Costs (2000 dollars)		
Project	Links to CCP Goal	Cost
Replace residences & office roofs (7 total)	13	$77,000
Replace phone lines (system)	13, 14	115,000
Replace two information kiosks	11, 14	40,000
Repair windmills, tanks, wells	1, 4-7, 10, 13	440,000
Repair water supply ditch (14 miles)	4, 9, 11, 14	140,000
Repair public use gravel roads (5.4 miles)	11, 13-15	27,000
Replace east storage building	13	235,000
Repair water control structures (8)	1, 4, 9, 13, 15	80,000

Appendix E. Compatibility Determinations

Station Name: Crescent Lake National Wildlife Refuge

Date Established: 1931

Establishing and Acquisition Authorities: Executive Order No. 5579 of March 16, 1931

Purposes for which Refuge was established:
". . . reserved and set apart . . . as a refuge and breeding ground for birds and wild animals."

". . . for use as an inviolate sanctuary, or for any other management purpose, for migratory birds" 16 USC § 715D (Migratory Bird Conservation Act).

National Wildlife Refuge System Mission: The mission of the National Wildlife Refuge System is "to administer a national network of lands and waters for the conservation, management, and where appropriate, restoration of fish, wildlife, and plant resources and their habitats within the United States for the benefit of present and future generations of Americans."

Description of Proposed Use:
Wildlife Observation, Wildlife Photography, Interpretation, and Environmental Education

Public use of the Refuge is limited by poor access. Wildlife observation and photography are very small portions of the total use; however, this low visitation results in one of the prime features about the Refuge the public comments on most consistently, the peace and quiet, and the solitude that can be found here.

Interpretation and education are also limited by poor access. There are particular groups that visit the Refuge year-after-year, but their numbers are not great. It is a major undertaking for a class to visit the Refuge.

The CCP proposes to continue the above uses and improve interpretation through the following actions:
- Establish one or two interpretative walking trails.
- Construct pullouts on the current auto tour route to provide a safer locations from which to view the Refuge. Relocating the current auto tour route from the County road to a secondary Refuge road would be desirable but not affordable at this time.

Availability of Resources
Sufficient resources are available to continue present programs. The walking trails would require some additional funding. The auto tour route change would be dependent upon providing a road that is capable of supporting all classes of vehicles in fair weather. Therefore, adding pullouts seems to be the best approach at this time.

Anticipated Impacts of the Use
Some areas of the Refuge will receive slightly higher use. It is not anticipated that this will adversely impact wildlife in any significant way.

Justification
Based on biological impacts described in the CCP and the Environmental Assessment, it is determined that wildlife observation, wildlife photography, interpretation, and environmental education within the Refuge will not materially interfere with or detract from the purposes for which the Refuge was established. Indeed, such activities are directly supportive of the Refuge purpose and provide opportunities to inform Refuge visitors about wildlife conservation and management and the National Wildlife Refuge System.

Determination
Wildlife observation, wildlife photography, interpretation, and environmental education are compatible.

Stipulations Necessary to Ensure Compatibility:
✓ The closed area where no public use at all is permitted will remain. This area provides almost complete freedom from disturbance for the most secretive of animals.
✓ Temporary closures and/or restrictions about exiting vehicles are tools that can be applied should such forms of public use prove detrimental to a particular species.

Description of Proposed Use: Fishing

Fishing is allowed in Island, Smith, and Crane Lakes. Island is open year-round, Smith and Crane Lakes are open only during the winter months. Use of boats is limited to Island Lake and gas powered motors are prohibited. Fishing is the most popular recreational activity on the Refuge, and occurs undiminished through most winters when ice cover permits.

The CCP proposes to continue the present uses but places an upper limit of 100 anglers per day on any body of water.

Availability of Resources
Sufficient resources are available to continue the existing fishing program. Crane Lake already has fish and will only require signs, parking access, and minor law enforcement activity. Limiting public use will probably not be necessary for many years. Use of options like reducing bag limits or catch-and-release regulations are tools that can be employed to limit use that would not require excessive staff effort as would more drastic measures like reservation systems.

Anticipated Impacts of the Use
Some wildlife disturbance is created by fishing activity. Disturbance during the summer is limited to Island Lake and mitigated by boat restrictions. Smith and Crane Lakes fishing causes almost no wildlife impacts since nearly all water-dependent wildlife migrates from the Refuge in the winter.

Justification
Based on the biological impacts described in the CCP and Environmental Assessment it is determined that recreational fishing within the Refuge will not materially interfere with or detract from the purposes for which the Refuge was established. Further, fishing has been identified as a priority public use in the National Wildlife Refuge System Improvement Act of 1997 when this activity is compatible with the Refuge purpose. However, should Smith or Crane Lakes winter-kill, an evaluation will be done by Refuge staff prior to any restocking of fish.

Determination
Recreational fishing as described is compatible.

Stipulations Necessary to Ensure Compatibility
✓ Crane and Smith Lakes open only in winter months.
✓ Motor and boat restrictions.
✓ Limit total anglers to 100 per day on any one body of water.

Description of Proposed Use: Hunting

At present, hunting is allowed on the Refuge for deer and upland birds. Hunting is second in popularity only to fishing. The opening of deer season is the highest public use day on the Refuge. The CCP proposes to continue the present uses and add waterfowl hunting at one lake.

The plan also proposes to limit peak hunter numbers to not more than 150 hunters per day.

Availability of Resources
Resources are currently available for the present hunting program. To add one new use will only require a change in the brochures and a limited amount of additional law enforcement since the season will be concurrent with existing seasons.

Anticipated Impacts of the Use
Hunting removes individual animals from the population and causes some wildlife disturbance. This disturbance is limited to fall and winter months when most wildlife have completed critical life processes and are migrating or absent from the Refuge. State and Federal game harvest regulations are in effect to assure perpetual populations of game animals and to also prevent populations from reaching unreasonable numbers resulting in die-offs or nuisance problems.

Justification
Based on biological impacts described in the CCP and Environmental Assessment it is determined that recreational hunting within the Refuge will not materially interfere with or detract from the purposes for which the Refuge was established. Further, hunting has been identified as a priority public use in the National Wildlife Refuge System Improvement Act of 1997 when this activity is compatible with the Refuge purpose.

Determination
Hunting as described is **compatible.**

Stipulations Necessary to Ensure Compatibility
✓ The present closed area to remain in effect to provide wildlife viewing opportunity even during open seasons.
✓ Limit peak numbers of hunters to a maximum of 150 on any given day. Reaching this limit is probably well into the future, but it will ensure that the basic quality of solitude will not be severely compromised.

Description of Proposed Use: Economic Management Tools (Grazing and Haying)

Current management activities that employ tools with an economic impact will be continued. Because of the annual bidding process as currently in practice, the refuge manager has complete control of these tools to use in a manner most effective for habitat improvement.

There are no changes in the current uses of these tools proposed in the CCP, other than replacing livestock with bison in the proposed wilderness unit.

Anticipated Impacts of the Use
Grazing and haying are used exclusively for the maintenance or improvement of habitat. The refuge manager has the flexibility to use these tools only as necessary, therefore, all impacts of these uses should be beneficial.

Replacement of livestock with bison will have impacts upon the grassland habitat in the proposed Wilderness Area. The CCP and Environmental Assessment discuss these impacts. It is anticipated that these impacts can be minimized through management and that the aesthetic and scientific benefits of such a natural situation will outweigh any slight habitat degradation.

Justification
Upland habitat would deteriorate without the use of a full range of management tools. Grasslands have evolved with fire and grazing which maintain the vigor of the habitat. Those wildlife species dependent upon grassland types not provided on commercially used rangeland find less and less habitat available, and maintenance of habitat quality on the Refuge is imperative.

Determination
Grazing and haying are compatible.

Stipulations Necessary to Ensure Compatibility
✓ General and specific conditions are required for each permit to ensure consistency with management objectives.

Signatures:

_____   Date _August 12, 2002_
Project Leader

Concurrence:

_____   Date _8-15-02_
Refuge Supervisor

_____   Date _8/15/02_
Regional Chief
National Wildlife Refuge System

Appendix F. Crescent Lake National Wildlife Refuge Species Lists

Birds

Names are in accordance with the American Ornithological Union check list. Birds known to nest on the refuge are marked with a closed dot (●). Those suspected to nest at least occasionally, but needing further confirmation, are marked with an open dot (○).

Loons
Common Loon — *Gavia immer*

Grebes
● Pied-billed Grebe — *Podilymbus podiceps*
  Horned Grebe — *Podiceps auritus*
● Eared Grebe — *Podiceps nigricollis*
● Western Grebe — *Aechmophorus occidentalis*
  Clark's Grebe — *Aechmophorus clarkii*

Pelicans
American White Pelican — *Pelecanus erythrorhynchos*

Cormorants
● Double-crested Cormorant — *Phalacrocorax auritus*

Bitterns, Herons, and Eagles
● American Bittern — *Botaurus lentiginosus*
  Least Bittern — *Ixobrychus exilis*
● Great Blue Heron — *Ardea herodias*
  Great Egret — *Ardea alba*
  Snowy Egret — *Egretta thula*
  Little Blue Heron — *Egretta caerulea*
  Cattle Egret — *Bubulcus ibis*
  Green Heron — *Butorides virescens*
● Black-crowned Night-Heron — *Nycticorax nycticorax*
  Yellow-crowned Night-Heron — *Nycticorax violacaceus*

Ibis, Stork
White-faced Ibis — *Plegadis chihi*

New World Vultures
● Turkey Vulture — *Cathartes aura*

Swans, Geese and Ducks
● Trumpeter Swan — *Cygnus buccinator*
  Tundra Swan — *Cygnus columbianus*
  Greater White-fronted Goose — *Anser albifrons*
  Snow Goose — *Chen caerulescens*
  Ross' Goose — *Chen rossii*
  Brant — *Branta leucopsis*
● Canada Goose — *Branta canadensis*
○ Wood Duck — *Aix sponsa*
● Gadwall — *Anas strepera*
● American Wigeon — *Anas americana*
  American Black Duck — *Anas rubripes*
● Mallard — *Anas platyrhynchos*
● Blue-winged Teal — *Anas discors*
● Cinnamon Teal — *Anas cyanoptera*
● Northern Shoveler — *Anas clypeata*
● Northern Pintail — *Anas acuta*
● Green-winged Teal — *Anas crecca*
● Canvasback — *Aythya valisineria*
● Redhead — *Aythya americana*
  Ring-necked Duck — *Aythya collaris*
  Greater Scaup — *Aythya marila*
● Lesser Scaup — *Aythya affinis*

  Long-tailed Duck — *Clangula hyemalis*
  Surf Scoter — *Melanitta perspicillata*
  White-winged Scoter — *Melanitta fusca*
  Bufflehead — *Bucephala albeola*
  Common Goldeneye — *Bucephala clangula*
  Barrow's Goldeneye — *Bucephala islandica*
  Hooded Merganser — *Lophodytes cucullatus*
  Common Merganser — *Mergus merganser*
  Red-breasted Merganser — *Mergus serrator*
● Ruddy Duck — *Oxyura jamaicensis*

Osprey, Kites, Hawks, and Eagles
  Osprey — *Pandion haliaetus*
● Bald Eagle — *Haliaeetus leucocephalus*
● Northern Harrier — *Circus cyaneus*
  Sharp-shinned Hawk — *Accipiter striatus*
  Cooper's Hawk — *Accipiter cooperii*
  Northern Goshawk — *Accipiter gentilis*
  Red-shouldered Hawk — *Buteo lineatus*
  Broad-winged Hawk — *Buteo platypterus*
● Swainson's Hawk — *Buteo swainsoni*
● Red-tailed Hawk — *Buteo jamaicensis*
○ Ferruginous Hawk — *Buteo regalis*
  Rough-legged Hawk — *Buteo lagopus*
  Golden Eagle — *Aquila chrysaetos*

Falcons and Caracaras
● American Kestrel — *Falco sparverius*
  Merlin — *Falco columbarius*
  Gryfalcon — *Falco rusticolus*
  Peregrine Falcon — *Falco peregrinus*
  Prairie Falcon — *Falco mexicanus*

Gallinaceous Birds
  Gray Partridge — *Perdix perdix*
● Ring-necked Pheasant — *Phasianus colchicus*
● Sharp-tailed Grouse — *Tympanuchus phasianellus*
  Greater Prairie-Chicken — *Tympanuchus cupido*
  Northern Bobwhite — *Colinus virginianus*

Rails
  Black Rail — *Laterallus jamaicensis*
● Virginia Rail — *Rallus limicola*
● Sora — *Porzana carolina*
● American Coot — *Fulica americana*

Cranes
  Sandhill Crane — *Grus canadensis*

Plovers
  Black-bellied Plover — *Pluvialis squatarola*
  American Golden Plover — *Pluvialis dominica*
  Semipalmated Plover — *Charadrius semipalmatus*
  Piping Plover — *Charadrius melodus*
● Killdeer — *Charadrius vociferus*

Stilts and Avocets
● American Avocet — *Recurvirostra americana*
● Black-necked Stilt — *Himantopus mexicanus*

Sandpipers and Phalaropes
  Greater Yellowlegs — *Tringa melanoleuca*
  Lesser Yellowlegs — *Tringa flavipes*
  Solitary Sandpiper — *Tringa solitaria*
● Willet — *Catoptrophorus semipalmatus*
○ Spotted Sandpiper — *Actitis macularia*
○ Upland Sandpiper — *Bartramia longicauda*
  Whimbrel — *Numenius phaeopus*
  Long-billed Curlew — *Numenius americanus*
  Hudsonian Godwit — *Limosa haemastica*
  Marbled Godwit — *Limosa fedoa*
  Red Knot — *Calidris canutus*

	Sanderling	*Calidris alba*
	Semipalmated Sandpiper	*Calidris pusilla*
	Western Sandpiper	*Calidris mauri*
	Least Sandpiper	*Calidris minutilla*
	White-rumped Sandpiper	*Calidris fuscicollis*
	Baird's Sandpiper	*Calidris bairdii*
	Pectoral Sandpiper	*Calidris melanotos*
	Dunlin	*Calidris alphina*
	Stilt Sandpiper	*Calidris himantopus*
	Short-billed Dowitcher	*Limnodromus griseus*
	Long-billed Dowitcher	*Limnodromus scolopaceus*
●	Common Snipe	*Gallinago gallinago*
●	Wilson's Phalarope	*Phalaropus tricolor*
	Red-necked Phalarope	*Phalaropus lobatus*

Skuas, Jaegers, Gulls, and Terns

	Franklin's Gull	*Larus pipixcan*
	Bonaparte's Gull	*Larus philadelphis*
	Ring-billed Gull	*Larus delawarensis*
	California Gull	*Larus californicus*
	Herring Gull	*Larus argentatus*
	Glaucous Gull	*Larus hyperboreus*
	Sabine's Gull	*Xema sabini*
	Caspian Tern	*Sterna caspia*
	Common Tern	*Sterna hirundo*
●	Forster's Tern	*Sterna forsteri*
	Least Tern	*Sterna antillarum*
●	Black Tern	*Chlidonias niger*

Pigeons and Doves

	Rock Dove	*Columbia livia*
●	Mourning Dove	*Zenaida macroura*

Cuckoos and Anis

○	Black-billed Cuckoo	*Coccyzus erythropthalmus*
●	Yellow-billed Cuckoo	*Coccyzus americanus*

Barn Owls

●	Barn Owl	*Tyto alba*

Typical Owls

●	Eastern Screech Owl	*Otus asio*
●	Great Horned Owl	*Bubo virginianus*
	Snowy Owl	*Nyctea scandiaca*
●	Burrowing Owl	*Athene cunicularia*
	Long-eared Owl	*Asio otus*
●	Short-eared Owl	*Asio flammeus*
	Northern Saw-whet Owl	*Aegolius acadicus*

Nightjars

●	Common Nighthawk	*Chordeiles minor*
	Common Poorwill	*Phalaenoptilus nuttallii*

Swifts

	Chimney Swift	*Chaetura pelagica*

Hummingbirds

	Hummingbird	*Archilochus spc*

Kingfisher

	Belted Kingfisher	*Ceryle alcyon*

Woodpeckers

●	Red-headed Woodpecker	*Melanerpes erythrocephalus*
	Yellow-bellied Sapsucker	*Sphyrapicus varius*
●	Downy Woodpecker	*Picoides pubescens*
	Hairy Woodpecker	*Picoides villosus*
●	Northern Flicker	*Colaptes auratus*

Tyrant Flycatchers

	Olive-sided Flycatcher	*Contopus borealis*
○	Western Wood-Pewee	*Contopus sordidulus*
	Eastern Wood-pewee	*Contopus virens*
	Willow Flycatcher	*Empidonax traillii*
	Least Flycatcher	*Empidonax minimus*
	Eastern Phoebe	*Sayornis phoebe*
○	Say's Phoebe	*Sayornis saya*
	Great Crested Flycatcher	*Myiarchus crinitus*
	Cassin's Kingbird	*Tyrannus vociferans*
●	Western Kingbird	*Tyrannus verticalis*
●	Eastern Kingbird	*Tyrannus tyrannus*

Shrikes

	Loggerhead Shrike	*Lanius ludovicianus*
	Northern Shrike	*Lanius excubitor*

Vireos

●	Bell's Vireo	*Vireo bellii*
	Solitary Vireo	*Vireo solitarius*
●	Warbling Vireo	*Vireo gilvus*
	Philadelphia Verio	*Vireo Philadelphicus*
	Red-eyed Vireo	*Vireo olivaceus*

Crows, Jays and Magpies

	Gray Jay	*Perisoreus canadensis*
●	Blue Jay	*Cyanocitta cristata*
	Pinyon Jay	*Gymnorhinus cyanocephalus*
	Black-billed Magpie	*Pica pica*
	American Crow	*Corvus brachyrhynchos*

Lark

●	Horned Lark	*Eremophila alpestris*

Swallows

	Purple Martin	*Progne subis*
●	Tree Swallow	*Tachycineta bicolor*
	Violet-green Swallow	*Tachycineta thalassina*
○	Northern Rough-winged Swallow	*Stelgidopteryx serripennis*
	Bank Swallow	*Riparia riparia*
●	Cliff Swallow	*Petrochelidon pyrrhonota*
●	Barn Swallow	*Hirundo rustica*

Titmice and Chickadees

●	Black-capped Chickadee	*Poecile atricapillus*

Nuthatches

	Red-breasted Nuthatch	*Sitta canadensis*
	White-breasted Nuthatch	*Sitta carolinensis*

Creepers

	Brown Creeper	*Certhia americana*

Wrens

	Rock Wren	*Salpinctes obsoletus*
●	House Wren	*Troglodytes aedon*
●	Marsh Wren	*Cistothorus palustris*

Kinglets

	Golden-crowned Kinglet	*Regulus satrapa*
	Ruby-crowned Kinglet	*Regulus calendula*

Thrushes

	Eastern Bluebird	*Sialia sialis*
	Mountain Bluebird	*Sialia currucoides*
	Townsend's Solitaire	*Myadestes townsendi*
	Veery	*Catharus fuscescens*
	Gray-cheeked Thrush	*Catharus minimus*
	Swainson's Thrush	*Catharus ustulatus*
	Hermit Thrush	*Catharus guttatus*
	Wood Thrush	*Hylocichla mustelina*

American Robin   *Turdus migratorius*
Varied Thrush   *Ixoreus naevius*

Mimic Thrushes
Gray Catbird   *Dumetella carolinensis*
Northern Mockingbird   *Mimus polyglottos*
Sage Thrasher   *Oreoscoptes montanus*
● Brown Thrasher   *Toxostoma rufum*

Starlings
European Starling   *Sturnus vulgaris*

Wagtails and Pipits
American (Water) Pipit   *Anthus rubescens*

Waxwings
Bohemian Waxwing   *Bombycilla garrulus*
Cedar Waxwing   *Bombycilla cedrorum*

Wood Warblers
Tennessee Warbler   *Vermivora peregrina*
Orange-crowned Warbler   *Vermivora celata*
● Yellow Warbler   *Dendrocia petechia*
Magnolia Warbler   *Dendrocia magnolia*
Black-throated Blue Warbler   *Dendroica caerulescens*
Yellow-rumped Warbler   *Dendrocia coronata*
Townsend's Warbler   *Dendroica townsendi*
Black-throated Green Warbler   *Dendroica Verens*
Blackburnian Warbler   *Dendrocia fusca*
Bay-breasted Warbler   *Dendrocia castanea*
Blackpoll Warbler   *Dendrocia striata*
Black-and-white Warbler   *Mniotilta varia*
American Redstart   *Setophaga ruticilla*
Worm-eating Warbler   *Helmitheros vermivorus*
Ovenbird   *Seiurus aurocapillus*
Northern Waterthrush   *Seiurus aurocapillus*
MacGillivray's Warbler   *Oporornis tolmiei*
● Common Yellowthroat   *Geothlypis trichas*
Wilson's Warbler   *Wilsonia pusilla*
Yellow-breasted Chat   *Icteria virens*

Tanagers
Scarlet Tanager   *Piranga olivacea*
Western Tanager   *Piranga ludoviciana*

Sparrows and Towhees
Green-tailed Towhee   *Pipilo chlorurus*
Western Towhee   *Pipilo erthrophalmus*
Cassin's Sparrow   *Aimophila cassinii*
American Tree Sparrow   *Spizella arborea*
Chipping Sparrow   *Spizella passerina*
Clay-colored Sparrow   *Spizella pallida*
Brewer's Sparrow   *Spizella breweri*
Field Sparrow   *Spizella pusilla*
● Vesper Sparrow   *Pooecetes gramineus*
● Lark Sparrow   *Chondestes grammacus*
● Lark Bunting   *Calamospiza melanocorys*
○ Savannah Sparrow   *Passerculus sandwichensis*
Baird's Sparrow   *Ammodramus bardii*
● Grasshopper Sparrow   *Ammodramus savannarum*
Fox Sparrow   *Passerella iliaca*
Song Sparrow   *Melospiza melodia*
Lincoln's Sparrow   *Melospiza lincolnii*
Swamp Sparrow   *Melospizaa georgiana*
White-throated Sparrow   *Zonotrichia albicollis*
Harris' Sparrow   *Zonotrichia querula*
White-crowned Sparrow   *Zonotrichia leucophrys*
Dark-eyed Junco   *Junco hyemalis*
McCown's Longspur   *Calcarius mccownii*
Lapland Longspur   *Calcarius lapponicus*
Chestnut-collared Longspur   *Calcarius ornatus*
Snow Bunting   *Plectrophenax nivalis*

Cardinals, Grosbeaks, and Allies
Northern Cardinal   *Cardinalis cardinalis*
Rose-breasted Grosbeak   *Pheucticus ludovicianus*
Black-headed Grosbeak   *Pheucticus melanocephalus*
● Blue Grosbeak   *Guiraca caerulea*
Lazuli Bunting   *Passerina amoena*
Indigo Bunting   *Passerina cyanea*
● Dickcissel   *Spiza americana*

Blackbirds and Orioles
● Bobolink   *Dolichonyx oryzivorus*
● Red-winged Blackbird   *Agelaius phoeniceus*
● Eastern Meadowlark   *Sturnella magna*
● Western Meadowlark   *Sturnella neglecta*
● Yellow-headed Blackbird   *Xanthocephalus xanthocephalus*
Rusty Blackbird   *Euphagus carolinus*
Brewer's Blackbird   *Euphagus cyanocephalus*
● Common Grackle   *Quiscalus quiscula*
● Brown-headed Cowbird   *Molothrus ater*
● Orchard Oriole   *Icterus spurius*
Baltimore Oriole   *Icterus galbula*
● Bullock's oriole   *Icterus galbula*

Finches
Purple Finch   *Carpodacus purpureus*
House Finch   *Carpodacus mexicanus*
Cassin's Finch   *Carpodacus cassinii*
Red Crossbill   *Loxia curvirostra*
Common Redpoll   *Carduelis flammea*
Pine Siskin   *Carduelis pinus*
● American Goldfinch   *Carduelis tristis*
Evening Grosbeak   *Coccothraustes vespertinus*

Old World Sparrows
● House Sparrow   *Passer domesticus*

Mammals

Shrews
Masked Shrew — *Sorex cinereus*

Moles
Eastern Mole — *Scalopus aquaticus*

Bats
Big Brown Bat — *Eptesicus fuscus*

Hares and Rabbits
Eastern Cottontail — *Sylvilagus floridanus*
Black-tailed Jackrabbit — *Lepus californicus*
White-tailed Jackrabbit — *Lepus townsendii*

Ground Squirrels
Thirteen-lined Ground Squirrel — *Spermophilus tridecemlineatus*

Pocket Gophers
Plains Pocket Gopher — *Geomys bursarius*

Mice and Rats
Plains Pocket Mouse — *Perognathus flavescens*
Silky Pocket Mouse — *Perognathus flavus*
Ord's Kangaroo Rat — *Dipodomys ordii*
Western Harvest Mouse — *Reithrodontomys megalotis*
Plains Harvest Mouse — *Reithrodontomys montanus*
White-footed Mouse — *Peromyscus leucopus*
Deer Mouse — *Peromyscus maniculatus*
Northern Grasshopper Mouse — *Onychomys leucogaster*
Bushytail Woodrat — *Neotoma cinerea*
Meadow Jumping Mouse — *Zapus hudsonius*

Voles
Prairie Vole — *Microtus ochrogaster*
Meadow Vole — *Microtus pennsylvanicus*

Muskrat
Common Muskrat — *Ondatra zibethicus*

Porcupine
Common Porcupine — *Erethizon dorsatum*

Coyote and Fox
Coyote — *Canis latrans*
Swift Fox — *Vulpes velox*
Red Fox — *Vulpes fulva*

Raccoon
Common Raccoon — *Procyon lotor*

Weasel and Mink
Long-tailed Weasel — *Mustela frenata*
Least Weasel — *Mustela nivalis*
Mink — *Mustela vison*

Badger
American Badger — *Taxidea taxus*

Skunks
Striped Skunk — *Mephitis mephitis*
Spotted Skunk — *Spilogale putorius*

Deer and Antelope
Mule Deer — *Odocoileus hemionus*
White-tailed Deer — *Odocoileus virginianus*
Pronghorn — *Antilocapra americana*

Extirpated
Black-footed Ferret — *Mustela nigripes*
Blacktail Prairie Dog — *Cynomys ludovicianus*
Elk — *Cervus canadensus*
Bison — *Bison bison*
Plains Grizzly Bear — *Ursus horribilis*
Plains Wolf — *Canis lupus*

Amphibians and Reptiles

Salamander
Tiger Salamander — *Ambystoma tigrinum*

Frogs and Toads
Woodhouse's Toad — *Bufo woodhousii*
Plains Spadefoot — *Spea bombifrons*
Western Chorus Frog — *Pseudacris triseriata*
Bullfrog — *Rana catesbeiana*
Northern Leopard Frog — *Rana pipiens*

Turtles
Common Snapping Turtle — *Chelydra serpentina*
Painted Turtle — *Chrysemys picta*
Yellow Mud Turtle — *Kinosternon flavescens*
Ornate Box Turtle — *Terrapene ornata*

Lizards and Skinks
Prairie Racerunner — *Cnemidophorus sexlineatus*
Lesser Earless Lizard — *Holbrookia maculata*
Many-lined Skink — *Eumeces multivirgatus*
Northern Prairie Lizard — *Sceloporus undulatus*

Snakes
Eastern Yellow-bellied Racer — *Coluber constrictor*
Plains Hognose Snake — *Heterodon platyrinos*
Bullsnake — *Pituophis catenifer*
Plains Garter Snake — *Thamnophis radix*
Red-sided Garter Snake — *Thamnophis sirtalis*

LIST OF HERBARIUM SPECIMENS
annotated and corrected by Steven B. Rolfsmeier,
2 October 1992 Note: This is not a complete list of flora at
Crescent Lake NWR.

DIVISION CHLOROPHYTA CHARACEAE
Chara sp.   muskgrass

DIVISION PTERIDOPHYTA
EQUISETACEAE   (Horsetail Family)
Equisetum laevigatum A. Br.   smooth scouringrush

DIVISION MAGNOLIOPHYTA
ACERACEAE   (Maple Family)
Acer negundo L.   box elder

ALISMATACEAE   (Water-plantain Family)
Alisma gramineum J. G. Gmel.   water plantain
Sagittaria cuneata Sheld.   arrowhead
Sagittaria latifolia Willd.   arrowhead

AMARANTHACEAE   (Amaranth Family)
Amaranthus arenicola. I.M. Johnst.   sandhills pigweed
Froelichia floridana (nutt.) Moq.   snake cotton

APIACEAE [UMBELLIFERAE]   (Parsley Family)
Cicuta maculata L..   water hemlock
Conium maculatum L.   poison hemlock
Sium suave Walt.   water parsnip

APOCYNACEAE   (Dogbane Family)
Apocynum cannabinum L.   Indian hemp, hemp dogbane

ASCLEPIADACEAE   (Milkweed Family)
Asclepias arenaria Torr.   sand milkweed
Asclepias incarnata L.   swamp milkweed
Asclepias speciosa. Torr.   showy milkweed

ASTERACEAE [COMPOSITAE] (Aster Family)
Ambrosia acanthicarpa Hook.   annual bursage
Ambrosia psilostachya DC.   western ragweed
Anthemis cotula L.   dog fennel
Artemisia campestris L.   western sagewort
Artemisia frigida Willd.   fringed sagebrush
Artemisia ludoviciana Nutt..   white sage
Aster Sp.
Bidens cernua L.   nodding beggar-ticks
Bidens frondosa L.   beggar-ticks
Bidens vulgata Greene   tall beggar-ticks
Chrysopsis villosa (Pursh) Nutt.   golden aster
Cirsium arvense (L.) Scop.   Canada thistle
Conyza canadensis (L.) Cronq.   horseweed, mare's tail
Erigeron bellidiastrum Nutt.   western fleabane
Euthamia gymnospermoides Greene   viscid euthamia
Helianthus maximilianii Schrad.   Maximilian sunflower
Helianthus petiolaris Nutt.   prairie sunflower
Iva xanthifolia Nutt.   marsh elder
Lactuca oblongifolia Nutt.   blue lettuce
Lactuca serriola L.   prickly lettuce
Liatris punctata Hook.   dotted gayfeather
Liatris squarrosa (L.) Michx.   smooth gayfeather
Lygodesmia juncea (Pursh) Hook.   skeletonweed
Machaeranthera linearis Greene   hoary aster
Palafoxia sphacelata (Nutt.) Cory
Ratibida columnifera (Nutt.) Woot. & Standl.
                                 prairie coneflower
Rudbeckia hirta L.   black-eyed susan
Senecio.tridenticulatus Rydb.   prairie ragwort
Shinnersoseris rostrata (Gray) Tomb   annual skeletonweed
Solidago canadensis L.   Canada goldenrod
Solidago missouriensis Nutt.   prairie goldenrod

Thelesperma filifolium (Hook.) Gray   greenthread
Townsendia exscapa (Richards.) Porter   easter daisy

BORAGINACEAE   (Borage Family)
Cryptantha fendleri (Gray) Greene   cryptantha
Lithospermum carolinense (Walt.) MacM.   hoary puccoon
Lithospermum incisum Lehm.   fringed puccoon

BRASSICACEAE   (Mustard Family)
Capsella bursa-pastoris (L.) Medic.   shepherd's purse
Lepidium densiflorum Schrad.   peppergrass
Lesquerella ludoviciana (Nutt.) S. Wats.   bladderpod
Rorippa palustris (L.).Bess.   bog yellow cress
Sisymbrium altissimum L..   tumbling mustard
Thelypodium integrifolium (Nutt.) Endl.   thelypody

CAMPANULACEAE   (Bellflower Family)
Lobelia siphilitica L.   blue lobelia

CAPPARACEAE   (Caper Family)
Cleome serrulata Pursh   Rocky Mountain bee plant

CAPRIFOLIACEAE   (Honeysuckle Family)
Symphoricarpos occidentalis Hook.
        western snowberry, buckbrush

CARYOPHYLLACEAE   (Carnation Family)
Saponaria officinalis L.   bouncing bet
Silene noctiflora L.   night-flowering catchfly

CHENOPODIACEAE   (Goosefoot Family)
Chenopodium album L.   lamb's quarters
Chenopodium rubrum L.   alkali blite
Corispermum nitidum Kit.   bugseed
Salsola collina Pall.   Russian thistle

COMMELINACEAE   (Spiderwort Family)
Commelina erecta L.   erect dayflower
Tradescantia occidentalis (Britt.) Smyth   spiderwort

CONVOLVULACEAE   (Morning glory Family)
Evolvulus nuttallianus R. & S.   evolvulus
Ipomoea leptophylla Torr.   bush morning glory

CUSCUTACEAE   (Dodder Family)
Cuscuta indecora Choisy   large alfalfa dodder

CYPERACEAE   (Sedge Family)
Carex atherodes Spreng.
Carex emoryi Dew.
Carex heliophila Mack.   sun sedge
Carex hystericina Muhl. ex Willd.   bottlebrush sedge
Carex interior Bailey
Carex lacustris Willd.   ripgut
Carex lanuginasa Michx.   woolly sedge
Carex nebrascensis Dew.   Nebraska sedge
Carex praegracilis W. Boott.   clustered field sedge
Carex scoparia Schkuhr ex Willd.   broom sedge
Carex stipata Muhl   sawbeak sedge
Cyperus engelmannii Steud.
Cyperus rivularis Kunth.   brook flatsedge
Cyperus schweinitzii Torr.   Schweinitz flatsedge
Cyperus strigosus L.   straw-colored nutsedge
Scirpus acutus Muhl.   hardstem bulrush
Scirpus maritimus L.   prairie bulrush
Scirpus pallidus (Britt.) Fern.   darkgreen bulrush
Scirpus pungens Vahl   three-square bulrush
Scirpus validus Vahl   softstem bulrush

EUFORBIACEAE   (Spurge Family)
Euforbia geyeri Engelm.   Geyer's spurge
Euforbia glyptosperma Engelm.   ridge-seeded spurge
Euforbia esula   (Schur) Soo   leafy spurge

FABALIEAE [Leguminosae]   (Bean Family)
Amorpha canescens Pursh   leadplant
Astragalus ceramicus Sheld.   painted milk-vetch
Dalea purpurea Vent.   purple prairie clover
Dalea villosa (Nutt.) Spreng.   silky prairie clover
Glycyrrhiza lepidota Pursh   wild licorice
Lathyrus polyamorphus Nutt.   hoary vetchling
Lotus purshianus Clem. & Clem.   prairie trefoil
Medicago lupulina L.   black medick
Medicago sativa L.   alfalfa
Melilotus alba Medic.   white sweet clover
Melilotus officinalis (L.) Pall.   yellow sweet clover
Psoralea lanceolata Pursh   lemon scurf-pea
Psoralea tenuiflora Pursh   wild alfalfa
Trifolium fragiferum L.   strawberry clover
Trifolium pratense L.   red clover
Trifolium repens   L.   white clover

HALORAGACEAE   (Water milfoil Family)
Myriophyllum exalbescens Fern.   water milfoil

IRIDACEAE   (Iris Family)
Sisyrinchium montanum Greene   blue-eyed grass

JUNCACEAE   (Rush Family)
Juncus balticus Willd.   Baltic rush
Juncus dudleyi Wieg.   Dudley rush
Juncus longistylis Torr.
Juncus torreyi Cov.   Torrey rush

JUNCAGINACEAE   (Arrowgrass Family)
Triglochin maritima   L.   arrowgrass

LAMIACEAE [LABIATAE]   (Mint Family)
Lycopus asper Greene   rough bugleweed
Mentha arvensis L.   field mint
Monarda pectinata   Nutt.   spotted beebalm
Nepeta cataria L.   catnip
Scutellaria galericulata L.-   marsh skullcap
Teucrium canadense L.   American germander

LENTIBULARIACEAE   (Bladderwort Family)
Utricularia vulgaris L.   common bladderwort

LILIACEAE   (Lily Family)
Allium textile A. Nels. & Macbr.   wild onion

LOASACEAE   (Stickleaf Family)
Mentzelia nuda (Pursh) T. & G.   stickleaf, sand lily

MALVACEAE   (Mallow Family)
Sphaeralcea coccinea (Pursh) Rydb.   scarlet globe mallow

NAJADACEAE   (Naiad Family)
Najas quadalupensis (Spreng.) Magnus   common naiad

NYCTAGINACEAE   (Four o'clock Family)
Abronia fragrans Nutt. ex Hook.   sweet sand verbena
Mirabilis glabra (S. Wats.) Standl.   smooth four o'clock

ONAGRACEAE   (Evening Primrose Family)
Calylophus serrulatus (Nutt.) Raven plains yellow primrose
Gaura coccinea Pursh   scarlet gaura
Oenothera latifolia (Rydb.) Munz   pale evening primrose
Oenothera nuttallii Sweet white-stemmed evening primrose
Oenothera villosa Thunb.   common evening primrose

PAPAVERACEAE   (Poppy Family)
Argemone polyanthemos (Fedde) G. Ownbey prickly poppy

PLANTAGINACEAE   (Plantain Family)
Plantago eriopoda Torr.   alkali plantain
Plantago major L.   common plantain
Plantago patagonica Jacq.   woolly plantain

POACEAE [GRAMINEAE]   (Grass Family)
Agrohordeum macounii (Vasey) Lepage   Macoun wildrye
Agropyron caninum (L.) Beauv.   slender wheatgrass
Agropyron cristatum (L.) Gaertn.   crested wheatgrass
Agropyron smithii Rydb.   western wheatgrass
Agrostis scabra Willd.   ticklegrass
Agrostis stolonifera L.   redtop
Andropogon hallii Hack.   sand bluestem
Andropogon scoparius Michx.   little bluestem
Aristida purpurea Nutt.   red three-awn
Bouteloua gracilis (H.B.K.) Lag. ex Griffiths   blue grama
Bouteloua hirsuta Lag.   hairy grama
Bromus japonicus Thunb. ex. Murr   Japanese brome
Bromus tectorum L.   downy brome
Calamagrostis canadensis (Michx.) Beauv.   bluejoint
Calamagrostis stricta (Timm.) Koel.   northern reedgrass
Calamovilfa longifolia (Hook.) Scribn.   prairie sandreed
Cenchrus longispinus (Hack.) Fern.   field sandbu
Dichanthelium acuminatum (Sw.) Gould & Clark
Dichanthelium oligosanthes (Schult.) Gould Scribner
panicum
Echinochloa muricata (Beauv.) Fern.   barnyard grass
Elymus canadensis L.   Canada wild rye
Eragrostis cilianensis (All.) E. Mosher   stinkgrass
Eragrostis trichodes (Nutt.)   Wood   sand lovegrass
Glyceria striata (Lam.) Hitchc.   fowl mannagrass
Hordeum jubatum L.   foxtail barley
Koeleria pyramidata (Lam.) Beauv.   junegrass
Leersia oryzoides (L.) Sw.   rice cutgrass
Muhlenbergia filiformis (Thurb.) Rydb.   pull-up muhly
Muhlenbergia mexicana (L.) Trin.   wirestem muhly
Muhlenbergia pungens ThUrb.   blowout muhly
Muhlenbergia racemosa (Michx.) B.S.P.   marsh muhly
Munroa squarrosa (Nutt.) Torr.   false buffalo grass
Oryzopsis hymenoides (R.& S.) Ricker   Indian ricegrass
Panicum capillare L.   witchgrass
Panicum virgatum L.   switchgrass
Paspalum setaceum Michx.   sand paspalum
Phleum pratense L.   timothy
Phragmites australis (Cav.) Trin. ex Steud.   common reed
Poa pratensis L.   Kentucky bluegrass
Sorghastrum nutans (L.) Nash   Indian grass
Spartina pectinata Link   prairie cordgrass
Sphenopholis obtusata (Michx.) Scribn   prairie wedgegrass
Sporobolus cryptandrus (Torr.) Gray   sand dropseed
Stipa comata Trin. & Rupr.   needle-and-thread
Triplasis purpurea (Walt.) Chapm.   sandgrass
Vulpia octoflora (Walt.) Rydb.   six-weeks fescue

POLEMONIACEAE   (Phlox Family)
Ipomopsis longiflora (Torr.) V. Grant   white-flowered gilia
Phlox andicola Nutt. ex Gray   plains phlox

POLYGONACEAE   (Buckwheat Family)
Eriogonum annuum Nutt.   grasshopper tobacco
Polygonum amphibium L.   water smartweed
Polygonum convolvulus L.   climbing buckwheat
Polygonum lapathifolium L.   nodding willow weed
Polygonum ramosissimum Michx.   knotweed
Rumex crispus L.   curly dock
Rumex.venosus Pursh   wild begonia

POTAMOGETCINACEAE (Pondweed Family)
Potamogeton illinoensis Morong Illinois pondweed
Potamogeton natans L. broad-leaved pondweed
Potamogeton pectinatus L. sago pondweed
Potamogeton richardsonii (Benn.) Rydb.
claspingleaf pondweed

PRIMULACEAE (Primrose Family)
Lysimachia thyrsiflora L. tufted loosestrife

RANUNCULACEAE (Buttercup Family)
Delphinium virescens Nutt. prairie larkspur
Ranunculus cymbalaria Pursh shore buttercup

ROSACEAE (Rose Family)
Potentilla norvegica L. Norwegian cinquefoil
Potentilla pensylvanica L. cinquefoil
Rosa arkansana Porter Arkansas rose
Rosa woodsii Lindl. western wild rose

RUBIACEAE (Madder Family)
Galium trifidum L. small bedstraw

RUPPIACEAE (Ditchgrass Family)
Ruppia occidentalis S. Wats. ditchgrass

SCROPHULARIACEAE (Figwort Family)
Agalinis tenuifolia (Vahl) Raf. slender gerardia
Penstemon albidus Nutt. white penstemon
Penstemon angustifolius Nutt. ex Pursh
narrowleaf penstemon

SOLANACEAE (Potato Family)
Physalis heterophylla Nees clammy ground cherry
Physalis hispida (Waterfall) Cronq. plains ground cherry
Solanum interius Rydb. plains black nightshade

SPARGANIACEAE (Bur-reed Family)
Sparganium eurycarpum Engelm. giant bur-reed

TYPHACEAE (Cat-tail Family)
Typha angustifolia L. narrow-leaved cat-tail
Typha latifolia L. broad-leaved cat-tail

URTICACEAE (Nettle Family)
Parietaria pensylvanica Muhl. Pennsylvania pellitory
Urtica dioica L. stinging mettle

VERBENACEAE (Vervain Family)
Verbena bracteata Lag. & Rodr. prostrate vervain
Verbena hastata L. blue vervain
Verbena stricta Vent. hoary vervain

ZANNICHELLIACEAE (Horned pondweed Family)
Zannichellia palustris L. horned pondweed

ZYOOPHYLLACEAE (Caltrop Family)
Tribulus terrestris L. puncture vine

Appendix G. Minimum Tools for Wilderness Management

The Wilderness Act of 1964 (Public Law 88-577/16 U.S.C. 1131-1136) defines wilderness as:

"A wilderness, in contrast with those areas where man and his works dominate the landscape, is hereby recognized as an area where the earth and its community of life are untrammeled by man, where man himself is a visitor who does not remain. An area of wilderness is further defined to mean in this Act an area of undeveloped Federal land retaining its primeval character and influence, without permanent improvements or human habitation, which is protected and managed so as to preserve its natural conditions and which (1) generally appears to have been affected primarily by the forces of nature, with the imprint of man's work substantially unnoticeable; (2) has outstanding opportunities for solitude or a primitive and unconfined type of recreation; (3) has at least 5,000 acres of land or is of sufficient size to make practicable its preservation and use in an unimpaired condition; and (4) may also contain ecological, geological, or other features of scientific, educational, scenic, or historical value."

The 24,502-acre proposed Crescent Lake Wilderness Area will be protected and managed so as to preserve its wilderness characteristics until such time as Congress acts on the proposal. The use of certain management tools is essential to maintain these characteristics. However, the use of those tools must be "minimized." Following is a brief description of those tools and their use. In the terms of management, all access into the Wilderness Area will be limited and the Refuge staff will avoid multi-trips. Specific management will be fully presented in the Wilderness Management Plan to be completed by May 2003.

Fire Management

The proposed wilderness is, and is surrounded by, a sea of volatile fuels; there is no road access to the perimeters adjacent to private lands. Thus, wildfires will be controlled by whatever means necessary to protect life and surrounding private property. Water supplies (including windmills) may be retained on the wilderness since there are no other reliable water sources. Motorized vehicles and other firefighting equipment may be temporarily stored on or near the wilderness to enable quick response.

Prescribed fires will be used only when essential to sustain wilderness characteristics. No more than 5 percent of the wilderness will be burned in any one year and the tools used will include all those needed to assure fires are contained within the planned burn areas and do not spread to surrounding private lands. This may include use of motorized vehicles such as pickup trucks, all-terrain vehicles (ATVs), tractors and mowers.

Grazing

Grazing may also be essential to sustain wilderness characteristics and, whether by cattle or bison, requires some supporting facilities and activities including: installation and maintenance of fencing; moving animals in, out, and within the wilderness; providing and maintaining water supplies; removing sick animals. All activities will be conducted without motorized vehicles when possible. When vehicles are necessary, ATVs will be used, whenever possible, to minimize physical impacts. No new water facilities are needed but removal of unnecessary wells and maintenance of others will require occasional use of heavier motorized vehicles. Electric fencing will be used occasionally to minimize the need for permanent facilities.

Control of Nonnative Plants

Biological controls have been implemented and will continue to be the tools of choice. However, monitoring indicates that Canada thistle continues to spread and that chemical control is also needed to maintain wilderness character. When chemical control within the wilderness is conducted, access will be by walking with backpacks (spot spraying in perimeter areas), and ATVs. Aerial spraying will be considered if needed to control large-scale invasions.

Public Use

All authorized public uses may occur within the wilderness to the extent they can be conducted without the use of motorized vehicles. However, solitude and primitive recreation is the overriding theme. Hiking, photography, and wildlife viewing will be allowed but no trails will be provided. Signs and interpretive facilities will be on the perimeters, outside the wilderness. There are no fishing lakes. Hunting will be permitted but the use of wheeled carts for removing game will not be allowed. The Nebraska Game and Parks Commission will be contacted in order to try to establish a special provision for the boning out of deer in the wilderness, which currently is prohibited by State law.

Appendix H. Species of Special Interest

Region 6 Species of Management Concern that Occur on the Refuge

American Bittern	*Botaurus lentiginosus*
White-Faced Ibis	*Plegadis chihi*
Trumpeter Swan	*Cygnus buccinator*
Northern Harrier	*Circus cyaneus*
Ferruginous Hawk	*Buteo regalis*
Upland Sandpiper	*Bartramia longicauda*
Black Rail	*Laterallus jamaicensis*
Long-billed Curlew	*Numenius americanus*
Black Tern	*Chlidonias niger*
Barn Owl	*Tyto alba*
Burrowing Owl	*Athene cunicularia*
Short-eared Owl	*Asio flammeus*
Redheaded Woodpecker	*Melanerpes erythrocephalus*
Loggerhead Shrike	*Lanius ludovicianus*
Dickcissel	*Spiza americana*
Lark Sparrow	*Chondestes grammacus*
Lark Bunting	*Calamospiza melanocorys*
Grasshopper Sparrow	*Ammodramus savannarum*
Eastern Meadowlark	*Sturnella magna*
Greater Prairie Chicken	*Tympanuchus cupido*
Yellow Mud Turtle	*Kinosternon flavescens*

State and Federally Listed

Endangered

Blowout Penstemon	*Penstemon haydenii*
American Burying Beetle	*Nicrophorus americanus*
Swift Fox	*Vulpes velox*

Threatened

Bald Eagle	*Haliaeetus leucocephalus*

Partners-in-Flight Watch List

Bobolink	*Dolichonyx oryzivorus*
Franklin's Gull	*Larus pipixcan*
Grey Catbird	*Dumetella carolinensis*
Black-billed Cuckoo	*Coccyzus erythropthalmus*

Appendix I. Step-Down Management Plans

Step-down management plans describe management strategies, procedures, methods and tasks for specific resources or functions. Step-down plans for Crescent Lake Refuge are listed below and are on file at the Refuge headquarters.

Approved Step-down Plans	Year Approved
Fire Management	1998
Fish Management	1980
Furbearer Management	1961
Hazard Communication	1996
Hunting	1969
Predator Management	1987
Water Management (Annual Plan)	2000
Wildlife Inventory	1995
Smith Lake Fishing	1996
(Amended to include Crane Lake)	2000
Integrated Pest Management	1995
Spill Prevention, Containment & Countermeasures	1999
Exposure Control - Blood Borne Pathogens	1997
Safety	1994
Signs	1999
Prescribed Burns (Annual Plans)	2000
Upland Mangement Plan	1996

Appendix J. Section 7

INTRA-SERVICE ENDANGERED SPECIES ACT SECTION 7 EVALUATION FORM

Originating Person: John F. Esperance, Branch Chief, Land Protection Planning

Telephone Number: 303-236-8145, ext. 658

Date: 07/11/02

Region: Region 6

III. Pertinent Species and Habitat:

A. Listed species and/or critical habitat within the action area:

blowout penstemon (E)   *Penstemon haydenii*
bald eagle (T)   *Haliacetus leucocephalus*

B. Proposed species and/or their proposed critical habitat within the action area:

None

C. Candidate species within the action area:

None

IV. Occurrence:

Prairie falcon, least tern, and piping plover are occasionally seen during migrations but are considered casual visitors. The ferruginous hawk is considered a sensitive species but is an uncommon migrant. Black terns and loggerhead shrikes are also sensitive species which nest on the Refuge.

The swift fox, an infrequent visitor, is a State listed species. One sighting was made on the Refuge in the year 2000.

The yellow mud turtle is a Refuge species of special interest.

V. Location:

The 45,849-acre Crescent Lake National Wildlife Refuge is located 28 miles north of Oshkosh, Nebraska in Garden County, within the Central Flyway, at the southwestern end of the Nebraska Sandhills.   It is administered as part of the Crescent Lake/North Platte National Wildlife Refuge

Complex. The Complex headquarters is 100 miles to the west in the city of Scottsbluff.

VI. Action:

The implementation of the Comprehensive Conservation Plan (CCP) is to facilitate the restoration, maintenance, and management of natural diversity. Additionally, the CCP facilitates continuity of management, and effective decision-making to achieve these ends. The Plan is intended to provide long-range guidance for the management of this Refuge based on careful consideration of the physical and biological characteristics of the land base. It is designed to facilitate achievement of the Service mission and Refuge goals which center on the protection and enhancement of wildlife and their habitats and the provision of appropriate compatible public recreation.

The Service has responsibility for stewardship over species that occupy Service lands and for the protection of cultural resources on these lands. Crescent Lake NWR, located in west-central Nebraska is a unique and ecologically important component of the National Wildlife Refuge System.

VII. Effects Determination and Response Requested

A. Listed Species

Not Likely to Adversely Affect, Beneficial effect - Concurrence requested on the proposed action

B. Proposed Species

No effect - Concurrence requested on the proposed action

C. Candidate Species

No effect - Concurrence requested on the proposed action

Steven A. Knode, Project Leader _____ Date __7/15/02__

    ☒ Concur   (Mark One)   [ ] Do Not Concur

    [ ] Formal Consultation Required   [ ] Conference Required

Remarks:

Appendix K. List of Preparers/ Review Team

This document is a compilation of efforts by Bill Behrends, (Refuge Manager, retired), Steve Knode (Project Leader), and Marlin French (Refuge Biologist). Dale Henry (ResPro Consulting) produced the written document in the approved format. Others involved in the process included: John Esperance (Planning) served as the Team Leader; Wayne King (Regional Biologist) provided guidance in developing the habitat and wildlife goals and objectives; Sean Fields (Planning) produced the maps; and Barb Shupe (Planning) completed edits and document layout.

Additionally, the following individuals formed the Review Team:

- Ken McDermond, FWS, Regional Chief of the National Wildlife Refuge System, Region 6
- Dave Heffernan, FWS, Deputy Regional Chief of the National Wildlife Refuge System, Region 6
- Larry Shanks, FWS, Refuge Supervisor (retired), Region 6/CO-KS-NE-UT
- Ron Cole, FWS, Refuge Supervisor, Region 6/CO-KS-NE
- Mike Spratt, Chief, Division of Refuge Planning
- Harvey Wittmier, Chief, Division of Realty
- Cheryl Williss, FWS, Regional Chief of Water Resources, Region 6
- Sheri Fetherman, FWS, Chief, Education/Visitor Services, Region 6
- Melvie Uhland, FWS, Education/Visitor Services, Region 6
- Rhoda Lewis, FWS, Regional Archaeologist, Region 6
- Dr. Jim Stubbendieck, Director, Center for Great Plains Studies, Univ. of Nebraska at Lincoln (UNL)
- Steve Riley, NGPC, Headquarters
- Dave Tunink, NGPC, Headquarters
- Bruce Morrison, NGPC, Headquarters
- Ritch Nelson, NGPC, Panhandle District Mgr, Wildlife Division
- Jack Peterson, NGPC, Panhandle District, Fisheries Supervisor
- Mark Lindvall, Neb. Chapter of The Wildlife Society
- Len McDaniel, FWS, Refuge Biologist (retired), Valentine NWR

The staff of the Crescent Lake National Wildlife Refuge wishes to thank all those involved in the preparation, review, and publishing of this Draft Comprehensive Conservation Plan.

Appendix L. Mailing List

Federal Officials
U.S. Senator Chuck Hagel, Washington, D.C.
 Mary Crawford, Ag Director, Scottsbluff, NE
U.S. Senator Ben Nelson, Washington, D.C.
 State Dir. W. Donald Nelson, Lincoln, NE
 Staff Assistant, Chadron, NE
U.S. Representative Tom Osborne, Washington, D.C.
 Esther Benson, District Office Director, Scottsbluff, NE

Federal Agencies
USDA/Natural Resources Conservation Service, Oshkosh, NE
US EPA, Denver, CO
USFWS, Air Quality Branch, CO; Albuquerque, NM; Alamos/Monte Vista NWR, CO; Anchorage, AK; Arapaho NWR, CO; Arlington, VA; Arrowwood NWR, ND; Atlanta, GA; Denver, CO; Des Lacs NWR, ND; Fort Snelling, MN; Hadley, MA; Juneau, AK; Ecological Services Field Office, Grand Island, NE; Fish Springs NWR, UT; Fort Niobrara/Valentine NWR, NE; J. Clark Salyer NWR, ND; Lost Trail NWR, MT; Medicine Lake NWR, MT; North Platte NWR, NE; Portland, OR; Rainwater Basin NWR, NE; Sacramento, CA; Sherwood, OR; Sand Lake NWR, SD; Seedskadee NWR, WY; Shepherdstown, WV; Upper Souris NWR, ND; Waubay NWR, SD
USGS, Biological Resources Division, Fort Collins, CO

State Officials
Governor Mike Johanns, Lincoln, NE
 Nancy Dunn, Dir. Field Operations, Western Office
State Senator Phil Erdman, Lincoln, NE

State Agencies
Nebraska Game and Parks Commission
 Ritch Nelson, Alliance, NE
 Jim Zimmerman, Alliance, NE
 Rex Amack, State Office, Lincoln, NE
Ash Hollow State Historical Park, Lewellen, NE
Nebraska State Historical Society, Lincoln, NE
Illinois Department of Natural Resources, Springfield, IL

Local Agencies
Garden County Commissioners
City of Oshkosh

Media
Star-Herald, Scottsbluff, NE
Gering Courier, Gering, NE
KNEB Radio, Scottsbluff, NE
KMOR/KOAQ/KOLT Radio, Scottsbluff, NE
Omaha World Herald, Omaha, NE
KDUH TV, Scottsbluff, NE
KSTF TV, Gering, NE
Garden County News, Jim McKeeman, Oshkosh, NE
Alliance Times-Herald, Alliance, NE
KAAQ Double Q Country FM

Libraries
Alliance Library, Alliance, NE
Oshkosh Library, Oshkosh, NE

Organizations, Business and Civic Groups
National Audubon Society, Washington, D.C.
Audubon Nebraska, Dave Sands, Lincoln, NE
Wildcat Audubon Society, Alice Kenitz, Gering, NE
Nebraska Chapter, TWS, Mark Lindvall, Valentine, NE
The Nature Conservancy
 Vincent Shay, Omaha, NE
 Doug Whisenhunt, North Platte, NE
The Nation Bison Assoc., Denver, CO
NE State Buffalo Association, Dave Hutchinson, Rose, NE
Rackett Fire District #1, Ashby, NE
Blue Creek Fire District #1, Lewellen, NE
North Platte Sportsman's Assoc, Keith Wiederspan, Oshkosh NE
Natl. Wildlife Ref. Assoc., Brent Giezentanner, Co Springs, CO
TWS, Central Mountain & Plains Section, Fort Collins, CO
Wildlife Management Institute, Rob Manes, KS; Bob Bryne, D.C.
KRA Corporation, F&W Reference Section, Bethesda, MD
Defenders of Wildlife, Washington, D.C.
The Wilderness Society, Washington, D.C.
Animal Protection Institute, Sacramento, CA
The Nature Conservancy, Boulder, CO
National Trappers Association, New Martinsville, WV

Universities & Colleges
University of Nebraska
 Thomas Bragg, Omaha, NE
 James Stubbendieck, Lincoln, NE
Ogalala Lakota College
 Don Althoff, Kyle, SD
Northwestern University, Professor Paul Friesema, Evanston, IL
University of Colorado, Shelly Drumm, Librarian

Individuals Expressing Interest in This Plan
Darrell Anderson	Dr. Stephen Kerr
Bill Behrends	Jim McGinley
Arnold Black, Jr.	Lynn Myers
Loren Blake	Dick Paisley
Cliff Buske	Jack Parker
Eddy Collins	Duane Petersen
Gerald DeWitt	Pat Peterson
Ev Dietlein	Hershell Rice
Tim Dietlein	Rush Creek Land & Livestock
Ron Dorman	Craig Schafer
Jim Ducey	Ron Shearer
Brad Emerson	Jim Snyder
Chancy Groves	Pat Thelander
Dale Henry	Todd Thies
Martin Hisel	Ted Turner, c/o Russell Miller
Dr. John Iverson	Ted Turner, c/o John Hansen
Kyran Kunkel,Ph.D.	Gale Young
Merle Jeffrey	Jack Zickefoose

Appendix M. Public Involvement / Consultation and Coordination

In the initial stage of CCP planning, a significant effort was extended to inform and solicit ideas from the public regarding a variety of Refuge programs and issues; open house invitations were mailed to 150 individuals on a mailing list comprised of local and national stakeholders (permittees, educators, neighbors and agency and non-profit organization representatives). An open invitation was further offered to interested parties via a widely published/broadcast news release. Both the personal and open invitations included requests to those unable to attend the open house but wishing to provide input into the planning process to contact the Refuge Manager for additional information and means by which to participate by mail.

The open house scoping session was held Thursday, July 16, 1998, from 2:00 pm until 7:00 pm at the Community Center in Oshkosh, Nebraska. The open house provided participants an opportunity to learn about the Refuge's purpose, mission and goals, and issues currently facing management. Fifteen people attended the afternoon/evening session and were provided the chance to speak with Service representatives and to share their comments. A summary of the most common issues is addressed below:

Bison

Several comments were received from the scoping meetings and from letters sent to the refuge manager about the possibility of reintroducing bison. Local ranchers were more concerned about the economics of having a government herd than the presence of the bison themselves. Some felt that having bison on the Refuge would compete with cattle producers for grazing. One comment was received about brucellosis. Other written comments were received supporting the idea of having bison on the Refuge.

This plan defines the concept of bison on the Refuge in terms of a privately-owned herd. This would be our first choice, should the concept proceed further. Should this idea move forward, it will require better boundary fences. Grants and/or donations would be needed in order to fund an enhanced boundary fence, so this alone would take some time to accomplish. Only cooperators who have disease free bison would be considered for a grazing permit.

A meeting with Nebraska Game and Parks Commission biologists in Alliance was held on November 9, 1998, to discuss this proposal. Issues and suggestions that surfaced at this meeting included:

1. *What will the impacts be to other wildlife?* This revolved around the fence that would be needed along the wilderness boundary. The refuge manager feels that a fence designed to permit deer and antelope to pass in and out of the wilderness would be required.

2. *Would the area have to be closed to access by hunters and hikers?* The refuge staff feels that the area would not have to be closed to access just because bison occur in the 24,500-acre proposed wilderness. Access is not restricted in Yellowstone or Theodore Roosevelt National Parks where bison roam freely. Part of the "wilderness experience" includes some inherent dangers but hunters and hikers should be able to visit the area with minimal risk.

3. *Would like to see "pre-bison" monitoring of the habitat and wildlife.* This is an excellent suggestion and will be done to some degree. The quality of the monitoring will be limited by funding and access limitations imposed by the Wilderness Act.

4. *Start small. Treat the bison like wildlife.* This was another good suggestion and the Refuge would be starting with a limited number of bison in a restricted area in order to determine if the herd is accomplishing our habitat goals and to see what problems arise with managing bison. While our initial intent was to have a government herd which we would treat as wildlife, there will be limitations on how "wild" a private herd can be.

A Bison Management Plan would need to be written before more details could be discussed.

Proposed Wilderness Area

The few comments we received about the wilderness during our scoping meetings were negative. Local Refuge users commented on the fact that losing vehicle access would cause a hardship for the old, the very young, and the disabled Refuge enthusiast.

The eastern one-half of the Refuge totaling about 24,500 acres was proposed as a wilderness in 1972. Independent of this planning process, it was brought to the attention of the refuge manager that U.S. Fish & Wildlife Service policy calls for a Proposed Wilderness to be treated as if it were a designated wilderness. Therefore, on September 1, 2000, the area was closed to public vehicle traffic and any management of the area by refuge staff will be done only when absolutely necessary and only with the "minimum tool" needed to accomplish the task. This policy will remain in effect until Congress acts on the wilderness proposal.

Fishing

The Refuge public use that generates the most use days is fishing. Comments at the scoping meeting dealt with increasing the number of walleye in Island Lake and expanding fishing opportunities by opening Crane Lake to fishing. Other comments included requests for "catch-and-release" fishing restrictions for bass and one complaint that the rail on the handicapped accessible fishing pier was too high.

Fisheries management on Crescent Lake Refuge is conducted by the Nebraska Game and Parks Commission staff out of Alliance, Nebraska. Management recommendations are offered to the refuge manager who, generally, approves the suggestion and the State implements their recommendation. The comment about stocking more walleye in Island Lake and the "catch-and-release" concept was passed on to the State fisheries biologist.

During the planning process for this document, the State had the opportunity to get yellow perch that could be stocked in Crane Lake. Our investigations indicated that an over abundance was occurring of fathead minnows in Crane Lake which added to the turbidity of the water. Stocking perch in Crane Lake would not only provide another fishing lake but would reduce the density of minnows and, hopefully, help clear the water. Clearer water will result in more submergent vegetation important to waterfowl and other wetland-dependent wildlife.

The refuge staff looked in to the height requirements for the handicapped railing on the fishing pier and found that it was built at the proper height.

County Access Road

It's been said that Garden County is the only County in Nebraska without a paved north/south road. Public comments about the current single lane road being in rough shape were, and are, common. The U.S. Fish & Wildlife Service assisted Garden County Commissioners in developing a proposal to improve the road utilizing Federal Highway monies. The County was successful in obtaining funding for a small portion of the needed repairs; however, substantially more money is needed in order to provide a road that Refuge visitors and the local residents could use dependably.

One suggestion that surfaced at the scoping meeting was that poison be used along the Refuge portion of the County road to reduce the kangaroo rats that burrow under the asphalt portions of the road. The refuge manager feels this would not be appropriate for a national wildlife refuge and feels that it would not be effective, given that as kangaroo rats are killed, others will quickly fill the void.

Civilian Conservation Corps (CCC)

One letter was received asking that the CCC (and WPA) structures and history be maintained. The Refuge staff is proud of the accomplishments of the CCC and fully intend to keep their historic efforts alive. Refuge managers will continue to make decisions at Crescent Lake Refuge with this in mind.

Managers met with several community groups during the ensuing weeks to further discuss the CCP process. Such groups included the Wildcat Audubon Society, Western Nebraska Sportsman Association, and the Scottsbluff Lions Club. The Crescent Lake/North Platte NWR Complex also conducted a formal staff meeting by which individual ideas were raised and documented regarding future refuge management direction.

Public Comments On Draft CCP

The Crescent Lake NWR Draft Comprehensive Conservation Plan and Environmental Assessment was released for a 30-day public review on May 1, 2002. The Service received 12 letters of comments from State and Federal agencies, private ranching community, private citizens, non-profit conservation group, and university officials. The Service received a number of editorial comments along with other substantial comments, which follow with our response.

Comment: One reader commented that the bison create blowouts which would benefit the endangered blowout penstemon.

Response: The Service agrees with the comment, and the text was added.

Comment: A comment on the strategy for reintroduction of bison was received saying that a wildlife biologist should be included in the Refuge Bison Advisory Council.

Response: The text was changed to include wildlife biologists.

Comment: One reader questioned the value of interseeding native grasses, as outlined in the document.

Response: After discussing the interseeding with a group of range specialists, we have removed this objective from the document.

Comment: A number of questions were asked about the total number of acres of blowout penstemon.

Response: The Refuge currently has 180 blowouts that historically have had penstemon. They average about 10 yards in diameter; some larger, some smaller. Of the 180 blowouts, we found 80 blowouts with penstemon in 2002. The Service added a sentence giving this information. Also, it was suggested that we monitor the success or any actions we take, with regards to penstemon. A sentence was added to emphasize this point.

Comment: Several comments were received about the bison issue. A comment stated that bringing in bison would be "a real mistake." This was based on observations of damaged grasslands by other bison herds in Nebraska. A concern was also stated about the cost of fencing needed to hold bison.

Response: Bison do graze differently than livestock and by starting small, evaluating and adapting, the Refuge plans to be able to manage our grasslands with bison. Bison could activate some blowouts, and while some would call this damaging the grassland, it also provides habitat for the endangered blowout penstemon plant. If bison are ever reintroduced to Crescent Lake Refuge, their impact on the area will be closely monitored.

There are a variety of types of fences used to confine bison throughout the United States. Some ranchers use multi-strand, high tensile electric fences. Others use standard barbed wire fences. Bison ranchers are developing new fence designs each year so if bison are reintroduced, a fence will be built that minimizes the impact to resident wildlife, will be economical to build and, most importantly, keeps the bison on Refuge lands.

Comment: Comments were received from the Nebraska Game and Parks Commission requesting that we consider adding opportunities to hunt more than just waterfowl.

Response: The Refuge is currently open to deer hunting and upland bird hunting and we have identified limited waterfowl hunting as a compatible recreational hunt. During the writing of a new hunt plan for the Refuge, we will work with Nebraska Game and Parks Commission biologists to examine further hunting opportunities.

Comment: With the assistance of Dr. John Iverson, quite a bit of information was added about the yellow mud turtle.